Your Compass to Living Your

one

Life to the Fullest

Cornelius Boersch, PhD, Crina Ancuta, MD & Dorina Serban, EMBA

Castle Mount
Media

2024

CASTLE MOUNT MEDIA GMBH & CO. KG
Burgbergstr. 94c
91054 Erlangen
Germany
https://castlemountmedia.com

Bibliographic information for the German National Library can be found under:
http://dnb.d-nb.de

Printed in Europe, the United States of America, the United Kingdom, Australia, and India.
Book Cover by Zeynep Burcu Tokatli
Book Design by Zeynep Burcu Tokatli and Florin Darie
Illustrations by Philip Behrends and Zeynep Burcu Tokatli
Editing by Howard VanEs, Let's Write Books, Inc.
Proofreading by First Editing

"Every page delivers a powerfully authentic perspective on life, both personally and professionally. For entrepreneurs, the lessons are mission critical. This book will enable you to realize the potential you might not even know you possess. It did for me!"

— **Jillian Manus, Silicon Valley Investor in Innovation Disruption and Diplomacy**

"This book goes beyond the glossy facade of success, delving into the essential layers that form the foundation of true achievement. The authors brilliantly dissect the concept of success, emphasizing the importance of understanding one's purpose, cultivating meaningful relationships, and investing in personal growth. This is not just another book about how to become financially successful; it's a guide to living a fulfilling and genuinely successful life. The insights offered in this book are invaluable for anyone looking to navigate the complex journey of entrepreneurship while staying true to themselves. A truly inspiring read."

— **Julian Teicke, Serial Entrepreneur and Investor, Founder and CEO of wefox**

„Inspiring, thought-provoking, and based on an abundance of experience. Worthwhile reading."

— **Karl-Theodor (KT) zu Guttenberg, Investor, Adviser, Author and Former Minister of Defence of Germany**

"In 'ONE,' Conny, Crina, Dorina and their guests offer a masterful blend of research-backed insights and practical guidance, empowering entrepreneurs to thrive in both their personal and professional lives. This book is a testament to the human potential, offering a roadmap for purposeful living, conscious relationships, and impactful entrepreneurship."

— **Katherine Woodward Thomas, New York Times Bestselling Author of**
Conscious Uncoupling & Calling in "The One"

"I have found the secret path to success as a world champion in kickboxing and a founder of 22 ventures, many of which have become international leaders. No one provides a better map of this path and shares what it takes to walk it than this book. It prepares you mentally, physically, and strategically, while at the same time fuelling your fire in the belly to just go out and do it."

— **Ola Ahlvarsson, Entrepreneur, Investor and Thought leader**

"Thoughts are gifts you have forever! - This book is like a gift shop for success and happiness."

— **Thomas Hessler, Investor in 200+ startups and Explorer in Crypto, Tech & Happiness**

"Read this book. Whether you want to become an entrepreneur or not, this book can help you direct your life and achieve your goals. After all, you only have one shot at life, Conny Boersch's story can be your guide to a life to live with purpose, a life with direction, a life you can live for the journey. You want to look back at your life when you become 70 and smile. This book can help you get there."

— **Tim Draper, Venture capital investor, and founder of Draper Fisher Jurvetson,**
Draper University and Draper Venture Network

„This book combines the essential of about 20 counselling books - a great guide towards personal success and happiness."

— **Dr. Tobias Reichmuth, serial entrepreneur and investor in the fields of the energy transition, crypto currencies, longevity and Switzerland's Shark Tank (Höhle der Löwen).**

CONTENTS

We have only one life.
one
So, we better make it right!

Introduction

We are inviting you to embark on a life-changing journey of self-discovery and personal development. You will not only read and learn from the best in their respective fields, but you will also be guided to become the best version of yourself!

We wrote this book for young entrepreneurs on a journey to become successful and who want to start performing at their best from the first attempt. We also had in mind established entrepreneurs struggling to bring together business success with family life, fun, and happiness. Just as important, this book can also be a valuable resource for people with remarkable business achievements, who are nudged by a sense of dissatisfaction, wondering if that is all that life has to offer . . .

We can only be happy and give our best if we live full, rounded lives, expressing all our gifts and taking care of everything that matters. We are more than a job title, a social status, or a bank account. Everything is interconnected. We cannot be successful entrepreneurs if we neglect our body, mind, and emotional health. Pursuing our business ventures becomes very difficult if we aren't financially savvy, if we ignore the environment we live in, and if we don't build supportive networks around us. All the money and fame in the world will soon become meaningless without a deep human connection with the people who matter most-friends, family, and partners. And because we are choosing this entrepreneurship path, we need to consider the impact we want to have in the world and on our planet.

The biggest struggle we had at the beginning of writing this book was identifying the ten most important areas of a fulfilled life and what to highlight in each area. There were so many topics and insights to consider that we had to zero in on what was truly most important to a fulfilled life. Otherwise, we would have ended up with an encyclopaedia. And perhaps one day, we will write one!

We will take you on a journey through the main areas of life, from entrepreneurship and impact in the world to happiness and everything in between. By taking this 360-degree view of life, you will notice the areas you have deprioritised and find the energy to re-open that chapter of your life, taking steps towards the dream you always had to postpone.

This book's purpose is to provide you with some of the latest knowledge for living your best life, as well as practical insights which have made a difference for us and in the lives of many people around us.

Meet Your Guides

ONE is the brainchild of Conny Boersch, a serial tech entrepreneur, political advisor, and tech investor, and Dorina Serban, an entrepreneur and angel investor passionate about personal development, mindfulness, and spirituality. Together, they have partnered with Crina Ancuta, an executive coach and medical doctor with twenty years of leadership experience, to create more than a book - a compass, a toolbox, and inspiration for entrepreneurs.

Hi, I'm Conny,

I am a serial entrepreneur and investor, of German origin, living between Zurich and Mallorca, a father, and a partner, merging three lives: tech entrepreneur, political advisor, and tech investor. I have invested in more than 400 companies globally since 1996, and in this book, I want to share with you what I learned in three decades of being an entrepreneur as well as everything that made me successful. And perhaps most importantly, what has made me a happy person, because I believe you can achieve anything you want when you're ambitious and curious enough to learn and grow every day!

In my twenty-five years as an investor, I have mentored and coached hundreds of entrepreneurs, some of them up to the unicorn level, and I have learned so much! The older I got, the more I realised how selfish it would be to keep all of these valuable lessons for myself and the ones close to me. So, I started working on this book together with my coach, Crina Ancuta, and with Dorina Serban, who inspired me to write this book. In our weekly sessions, Crina asked me the right questions, challenged me, gave me advice, made critical comments, and helped me structure my ideas and think more clearly. At the age of fifty-five, this book became not just a summary of insights and learnings but a valuable personal growth resource I can rely on.

I believe that the way we prepare our kids to manage life is not adequate anymore, and the way we prepare young founders to be successful and happy entrepreneurs is a disaster. In school and university, we learn important aspects of science, business, or law, but nobody is teaching us "how to live an amazing life." We expect our parents to give us this wisdom, and there is only so much two people can do, irrespective of the gifts they have or the time they invest in their kids' education.

Relying just on your family and school education when there is so much knowledge available out there in the world is a huge limitation! Still, it is difficult to find relevant, accessible information from trustworthy sources. That is why we decided to put together the best findings of our journeys with the experience of people we admire the most and the best research-validated insights and practices in one book, to give you a summary of best practices with the tools to transform your life.

In my life, I have seen how important it can be to have the right advice at the right time. And I regret that often, I did not listen even to the people I looked up to. I wasn't always the confident, funny, and charming person I am today. My life changed when, at the age of fourteen, my father gave me the twelve tapes of Dennis Waitley's The Psychology of Winning: Ten Qualities of a Total Winner, where he shares the results of researching the most successful people in America and identifies what patterns and behaviours they have in common. I was very good at football, but very bad in school, and suffered from dyslexia.

Back in those days, my teacher thought I was stupid, and my parents should be happy if I finished any level of school. But I started to listen to the tapes, repeatedly, over months and years. I became more ambitious. I started to ask myself: What do I want to achieve? What do I want my life to become? I changed my habits and tried to implement everything I learned into my life, every day. Over the years, I became better and better. I graduated from university, did my PhD in venture capital, and became an honorary professor in entrepreneurship. And along the way, I wrote seven books. More importantly, I became a super-happy person.

The ultimate goal for all of us is to have a happy and fulfilled life. For me, happiness is more an attitude than an objective reality. Happiness has little to do with money. But not having money can be very challenging, to say the least! Success in business gives you financial independence and a certain degree of freedom. And the power to make a difference in the world!

I was always fascinated when I met billionaires from all over the world: so many of them were very unhappy or had a fulfilled life in only one or two areas. This was also true of the many successful entrepreneurs I got to know during my career: they excelled in business and networking but were neglecting their health, relationships, or personal growth. Of course, everyone defines success in life differently. In my view, I believe that someone truly successful is accomplished in business, contributing to society, and at the same time capable of conducting a healthy and happy private life where they enjoy life to the fullest.

Writing this book was like therapy for me. For months and months, I reflected on various aspects of my life. I thought about the key learnings - the big failures, the magic moments, the biggest worries. While working on the book, I learned so much, and many aspects of my life became clearer. This book is an important part of my life, and it has the potential to be a turning point in yours, too, if you allow it. So, see it as a friendly push from our side!

Hi, I'm Crina,

I'm an executive coach, guiding leaders through organisational (and personal) crises to build heart-centred foundations for sustainable growth and fulfilment. My mission is to assist them in creating a long-lasting legacy they can be proud to leave behind, as they live conscious, rewarding personal lives.

Romanian by birth, British by choice, and global citizen by human design, I've lived a few lives: from medical doctor to pharma executive, coach, and now writer, while raising two children as a single mother, adapting to various cultures, and always striving to be a better version of myself.

In 2012, when I visited the Mumbai slums during a senior executive training trip, sitting on the cement floor of a house half the size of my kitchen in the London suburbs, looking at the smile and generosity of our hosts, I understood that we, privileged citizens of the Western world, have lost the connection with what is most important in life. We complain about low-speed internet, slow traffic, and workplace conflicts, when less financially fortunate people smile with all their hearts just for being alive.

This started my journey of gratitude, my recovery from the pursuit of socially defined goals, feeling broken and complaining about life not giving me what I want. Back in the U.K., I had the epiphany that work should not define me. I was more than a senior director, more than an ex-partner, more than a single mother. There was something valuable inside me, in the deepest part of my soul, that no struggle will take away.

With twenty years in key local, regional, and global roles in the pharmaceutical industry, inspiring and developing people as a leader, mentor, and coach, I've experienced it all. I have led and transformed organisations, motivated and inspired teams to launch innovative treatments, created compelling strategies for business expansion, and orchestrated excellence in execution to improve the quality of life and survival of people living with debilitating diseases. I've achieved significant recognition for crisis management, performance acceleration, and cultural change. Behind the scenes, I have always been motivated by my own personal journey of transformation - being the *best mother for my children, adapting to different cultures, learning to navigate corporate politics, and trusting my business instinct.*

There has been one constant throughout my entire life: doing good for people. Immersed in performance, executive, and relationships coaching, and devouring leadership, human behaviour, neuroscience, and spirituality courses and books for a decade, I ended up developing a unique method of helping people. This highly effective multifaceted approach enables my clients to achieve remarkable results by optimising their mind-body-heart-soul connection and tapping into their greatness within. Combining positive intelligence and bio-hacking practices with conscious leadership principles and ontological coaching, it allows them to become the authentic, impactful, and compassionate business leaders our world needs today.

When my work brought Dorina, Conny, and myself together, I said yes to Conny's invitation to write a book that could change lives. For anyone who thinks, "I cannot have an impact on today's world unless I have a certain social status, education, race, gender, title or wealth," I have one simple message: #YESWECAN. It's time to stop living our lives blindfolded, running the same race, unaware of the possibilities that exist . . . for anyone, regardless of their station in life.

Allow this book to be the catalyst that will move you from breakdown to breakthrough, from surviving to thriving, from the old, limited self to the winner identity you were born with. I know you will surprise yourself with who you become once you commit to your growth journey! Using Mary Oliver`s words, let me ask you, "Tell me, what is it you plan to do, with your one wild and precious life?"

Hi, I'm Dorina,

I'm an entrepreneur, an angel investor, and, above all, a dedicated explorer of visionary ways to unlock new depths in human potential. My personal mission is to inspire and support people on their journeys to becoming the best version of themselves and making the most of their lives. Born in Romania, my professional career brought me to live in Germany, and I travelled the world before finding my home in Switzerland.

Holding an Executive Master's in Business Administration, I spent over a decade in the corporate healthcare world before deciding to become an entrepreneur. During this time, I led local and global commercial operations, empowering individuals to achieve success in their roles. Working in complex structures, leading multicultural teams through periods of change, and fostering connections with key medical opinion leaders around the world, I understood that true success requires a multifaceted approach. This realisation sparked my personal quest to explore and understand the tools for inner transformation that bridge the realms of science and ancient wisdom. When I found the courage to follow my heart, step out of my comfort zone, and become an entrepreneur, true transformation began to unfold in my life.

Over the past seven years, I have spent my time at the intersection between business, personal growth, and spirituality, connecting people with the right resources and opportunities, and supporting entrepreneurs in their journey. At the same time, I immersed myself in learning about personal transformation, completing an international certification in systemic constellations, and attending numerous workshops and conferences on topics like transpersonal psychology, neuroscience, bio-hacking, mindfulness, and holistic health. An area I currently have great interest in is the evolution of consciousness and the potential benefits of psychedelics in healing and personal growth.

While I was supporting Conny through his inner discovery, we realised that it took decades for him to develop his own personal practices for success - not knowing that top personal growth and spiritual teachers had been recommending similar tools for many years. At the same time, while becoming an entrepreneur myself and working with Conny, I experienced firsthand the difference his experience made in the lives of many entrepreneurs. So, we committed to bringing this knowl-

edge and a holistic approach to living our one life to other entrepreneurs, to guide and inspire them in their journey.

As George Bernard Shaw aptly put it, "Life isn't about finding yourself. Life is about creating yourself." We are all a work in progress, shaping who we are through experiencing, learning, and transforming, every day. By writing and compiling this book - reflecting on every aspect of life, curating relevant and practical resources, challenging each other, and having deep conversations with the amazing people featured in the book - we also continued to create ourselves. We warmly invite you to join us in this process and create the highest expression of yourself, each and every day.

How to Get the Most from This Book

In the beginning of every chapter, you will get a glimpse of Conny's world as he shares personal thoughts and experiences heard by his inner circle only. After that, we blend real-life insights from successful entrepreneurs, with transformative concepts and tools from leading experts, to provide you with a rich and accessible experience.

As you go through this book, keep in mind that there is no right or wrong way to begin. Start with the first chapter, or choose the chapter that calls to you first.

As with any expedition, though, it is a good idea to have a map of the territory, and before starting the journey (in this case, reading the chapters), you want to know exactly where you are now. To assist you with this, we have provided a questionnaire here: www.onelifenow.com/onelifeassessment. You'll get the most from this book by using the questionnaire, and we suggest that you fill it out when you are finished reading this introduction.

For each chapter, we recommend that you:

1   First, **have an inquisitive and curious mindset as you explore** the insights presented, gathered from the most enlightened minds of our time, as well as the reflections and life lessons from the successful entrepreneurs we interviewed.

2   Second, **find out where you are now** in that area of life, reflecting on what you read, along with your questionnaire assessment.

3   And third, as you read through each chapter, a**nswer the reflection questions provided and choose** the ideas and tools that resonate with you.

The book offers you:

Food for thought. You do not have to agree with every single piece of advice or comment. We only ask that you be open, test the ideas and tools we offer, and integrate what resonates with you in your daily routine or mindset.

Different perspectives people have when it comes to happiness or success. It also shows that there are various methods and ways to achieve it.

A powerful catalyst to **reflect on your life today and how you would like it to be in the future.**

CHAPTER ONE

Entrepreneurship Unfiltered:
Your Mindset Defines Your Success

"Man often becomes what he believes himself to be. If I keep on saying to myself that I cannot do a certain thing, it is possible that I may end by really becoming incapable of doing it. On the contrary, if I shall have the belief that I can do it, I shall surely acquire the capacity to do it, even if I may not have it at the beginning."

— Mahatma Gandhi

THE UNBELIEVABLE JOURNEY:
From Great Idea to Game Changer

On August 11 2023, I reached the peak of my journey as an investor. The company I created in 2021, Mountain & Co. I Acquisition Corp. (MCAA), entered into a definitive agreement with FC Barcelona to bring its content creation platform, Barça Media, to the U.S. and other global financial markets, in a transaction valued at approximately US$1 billion.

FC Barcelona is one of the most successful professional football clubs in the world, with more than 330 million fans and 434 million television viewers in the 2021-2022 season alone, as well as 421 million social media followers. The combination with Mountain & Co. I Acquisition Corporation would give Barça Media access to the U.S. capital markets , create an even stronger platform, and reinforce the club's digital transformation.

When impressive stories like this appear as front-page news in the media, what you actually see is the tip of the iceberg. Only the people behind the scenes can see how complex and bumpy the real journey towards closing a deal of such magnitude can be.

For this transaction, the journey began with a personal decision to challenge myself and attempt a project entirely different to the small start-up investments I was used to. I knew that simply repeating what made me successful in the past would not take me

A reluctance to take big risks had often held me back.

to the next level. I also admitted to myself that a reluctance to take big risks had often kept me from being as sucessful as I wanted to be.

With these new insights, I restructured my team, hired young talent, and surrounded myself with the best advisors with experience in large, uncertain projects. It was in this constellation that the idea of a SPAC was born.

Simply put, a SPAC is a special purpose acquisition company created solely to raise funds through an IPO to merge with or acquire an existing company. The SPAC sets out distinct criteria, which guide it towards finding a suitable target company within a specified time frame. Companies choose to merge with a SPAC to raise additional capital and become publicly traded more quickly, with reduced regulatory bureaucracy compared to a traditional IPO.

Our SPAC would be known as Mountain & Co. I Acquisition Corp. and trade on the NASDAQ as MCAA. We settled on an investment thesis focusing on bringing European technologies to a U.S. stock exchange

CHAPTER ONE

A billboard on Times Square announces the merger between Barca Media and Mountain & Co. I Acquisition Corp.

and began fundraising. Together with Credit Suisse, we quickly raised over US$200 million from some of the worlds's most renowned investors. They liked our ideas and track record, so they agreed to invest in European technology and have it listed on the stock exchange.

What differentiated us from other SPACs was primarily our team: we recruited prominent, experienced leaders like Philipp Rösler (former Vice Chancellor of Germany and former board member of the World Economic Forum), Utz Claassen (former CEO of multiple German corporations) and Thomas Middelhoff (former CEO of Bertelsmann Group). By combining their extensive managerial experience with strong personalities and sales acumen, we knew we could achieve anything we set our minds to. Never had I seen a group of exceptional people bring together such powerful energy to work towards a common goal.

Our team approached a large number of "target" unicorns (privately held start-ups valued at over US$1 billion) across Europe, but the investment climate was changing fast. Due to the complex set of requirements, most companies either didn't fulfil our criteria or the timing for such a transaction wasn't right.

Finally, in November of 2022, a famous investor contacted us, stating that he might have a suitable target company. However, he mentioned that there was a level of uncertainty about this target and that he was not sure if they would be even interested in this kind of deal. We were sceptical. We had received many such introductions. Then he shared the name: FC Barcelona, the world-famous football club. We learned that FC Barcelona was considering spinning off several digital revenue streams (like VR, fan tokens, AI, NFTs) into separate entities, and looking for partners who could help to accelerate each of them individually.

At this point, I asked myself, "What do I know about football?" While it is true that I became quite popular by playing the sport in high school, my professional expertise lies in tech companies, not football. What made this opportunity fascinating, however, was that this specific football club wanted to expand into my world - become more digital. This was exactly the kind of goal that my SPAC team and I were perfectly positioned to support.

After months and months of negotiating, the club realised they needed our SPAC due to the perfect alignment between their will to take a pioneering role in digital sports media, their desire to sustainably access the resources to compete at the highest level, and our team's skillset and resources. Together, with FC Barcelona's management, we determined that it would make the most sense for the club in the long run, if all digital business units were run as one entity. The more we dove into the project, the more interesting (and challenging!) it began to appear.

This deal was going to be very different from anything I had worked on before. First, our team had to understand how a football club worked, accepting that it's an untameable political beast. Next, we wouldn't be dealing with a single entrepreneur but instead with a club president, whose board members all voted and shared decision-making power. Furthermore, the football authorities would be telling us what we can do . . . while banks and lawyers would be telling us what we cannot do! Every little detail would need to be checked and approved by dozens of individuals and authorities.

What kept this project alive was that everybody wanted to make a deal: the football club, the authorities, the banks, our team, the investors, and even the lawyers . . . everybody wanted it. What nearly killed it several times - was that it was technically very, very difficult.

No matter what, our team kept going, and going, and going. For Thomas Middelhoff, my advisor, failure was not an option. The more I worked with him, the more I understood why he had been the successful CEO of a company with over 100,000 employees decades ago: his energy was just unbelievable.

Operations financing quickly became a focal point. While we had the backing of Credit Suisse and a list of great investors, we had to continuously inject more and more money into this project. Aware of the risk, I felt extremely uncomfortable, almost unsafe. For the first time in twenty years, I was struggling to pay the monthly bills, because I had to inject hundreds of thousands into the SPAC every month to keep operations running. Noticing the cash outflow from my account, even my bank officer called me to make sure I wasn't being blackmailed.

The key to success is learning how to manage conflicting emotions.

During this uncertain time, it was both encouraging and frustrating to hear from my coach and some of my friends that I needed to be "out of my comfort zone" to succeed. Despite my belief in success and my commitment to the project, there were many times when I questioned how sensible it would be to move forward. What weighed on me, in particular, was knowing that so many people were depending on me.

Looking back, I learned that the key to success in situations like these is learning how to manage conflicting emotions: balancing the fear you feel when taking a big risk with the excitement of the potential win in the future. Instead of allowing fear to take over, I focused on the belief that this transaction would work out.

Particularly difficult was the decision to sell off the right to a significant part of my future profits to new investors who leveraged the situation to get a good deal. This was very painful for me, but I kept reminding myself of the big picture. Ultimately, I knew it would be best to close the deal, even with a bruised *ego. If the overall damage of losing a deal is high, then wisdom - not ego - must dictate my actions.*

It sounds easy to tell someone to remain positive and "stretch your limits," but when you do this for long periods of time - and if you're not skilled at managing your mental, emotional, and physical energy - such situations will be difficult for

Perseverence is key, don't quit too early!

you, your family, and everyone else around you. That's because, during times like these, you turn into a different person. I know that I changed entirely because I wanted to win so badly. This drove me to focus on the SPAC day and night, seven days a week. I sacrificed most weekends and still felt pressure from all sides. Part of me felt as if I had been forced into working like this, and I could see no other option. As the CEO of this NASDAQ-listed company, all the responsibility and risks were ultimately on my shoulders.

For months, everything that could go wrong did go wrong! Not surprisingly, I couldn't sleep anymore - and when the alarm went off in the morning, I needed to manage my energy as best I could. I found that exercising and sauna were the only things that could take my mind off this transaction. When you have such a major issue on your hands, you cannot focus on anything else. You cannot even focus on your private life. That had to be parked for a while.

In the end, we accomplished much more than we ever expected - and it was worth it. I know that focusing on the fact that everybody wanted this deal got me through the most challenging times. Finally, I followed my own advice when it came to winning strategies I often give the entrepreneurs I coach and mentor: you may be experiencing difficulties, but don't quit too early - perseverance is key. I also hate losing, so that gave me the energy to wake up every day and start again. In the end, probably the most important lesson I learned from this experience is that everything is possible if you refuse to give up. Through it all, I realised that this transaction would be a game-changer in my own life.

— Conny

ENTREPRENEURS:

The Creators, Disrupters, and Innovators Who Improve the World

You may wonder why this book begins with the entrepreneurship chapter - and why this chapter receives so much space in the book. We believe that entrepreneurs are the ultimate engines of society; they drive innovation and new business practices, and they attract great talent. Entrepreneurship combines creativity and courage, resilience and resourcefulness, and strength and agility to create a new world - and if you're reading this book, we suspect that somewhere deep in your heart, you feel the same way.

Becoming an entrepreneur is a profound, life-changing decision. Oftentimes, it is also a one-way street from which there is no turning back. Not because you wouldn't be hired back into the corporate world, but because your mindset has shifted irreversibly. Once you've tasted the freedom and excitement that comes with being an entrepreneur, it's difficult to go back to being an employee.

Even though start-ups are a less mature, less stable, and (most of the time) less lucrative space, entrepreneurs are drawn to the challenges, and to the chance to make a big impact and exit one day as a multimillionaire.

Is it Worth It? The Pros and Cons

In this chapter, you will discover the raw, unfiltered reality of entrepreneurship from someone who has been in this scene for almost forty years. You will learn what it takes to succeed as an entrepreneur - information that you will not find in other books, at least not with this level of honesty.

Being an entrepreneur is a very powerful self-development exercise. The only limit holding you back is your ambition. Fortunately, once you experience success, you will realise that you can always repeat it. Become a serial entrepreneur, and you will improve with every business you start. However, not every day is a "win," and entrepreneurship is not always glamorous, either.

The PROS of being an entrepreneur

As an entrepreneur you can...

• Be your own boss: you can choose the business you want to create and the people you want to work with.

• Align your personal interests with your job.

• Develop a better connection between the input and output of your work (e.g., you can better predict the type of results you will achieve based on the effort you put in to the project); hence, there is a greater chance that you can foresee when and how you will succeed.

• Have a greater impact on the people around you, compared to being a small cog in a big machine.

• Enjoy unlimited potential to become wealthy!

The CONS of being an entrepreneur

As an entrepreneur, you will . . .

•   Never stop thinking. You work all the time, and you worry all the time. There will always be a "what if" on your mind, and therefore many sleepless nights.

•   Carry all the responsibility on your shoulders, and you will "take it to bed" every evening - which is often a challenge for your family life. That's why it's so important to love what you do and to find the right life partner capable of understanding and supporting you. When I started my entrepreneurial journey, I worked day and night. It took me seven years to realise I would die if I continued at that same pace. Don't make the same mistake I did!

•   Face constant pressure to remain ahead of the game - especially in tech, where you are often involved in a market that doesn't even exist yet. Timing is critical for start-up success.

•   Encounter criticism when you fail. Yet, you must handle failure constructively. This will be discussed later in this chapter, but I've never met someone who became successful without living on the brink of bankruptcy first. If you haven't tasted failure, you will rarely savour success.

The Sooner, The Better

When it comes to entrepreneurship, we want to stress the importance of starting very early. The sooner you start, the better. You can handle the pain and effort a lot better when you have less to lose (not to mention that it takes five to six years on average before you get any reward).

Daniel Krauss, one of the three founders of FlixBus, revealed at Unternehmertag in 2021 that his biggest regret in life so far is that he could have started his journey as an entrepreneur much earlier. He also added that "sometimes you really dedicate quite a lot of time to the company, and this is awesome to a certain extent. But you must not forget about your personal life. I wouldn't say this is a regret yet, but it's something I monitor very carefully." Statistics show that the most successful entrepreneurs are older. This is due to their years of experience, as they learn how to leverage what they discover after each failure to ultimately become successful.

If you already have a business, many of these pros and cons will likely be obvious. Yet, taking time to reflect on them gives you a good foundation for setting your vision with ambition and eyes wide open! Take a moment to reflect on where you've been, where you currently are, and where you want to go with your business:

Reflection Questions

- What is your vision for the business you want to create?

- What product(s)/service(s) do you want to develop?

- Who are the people you want to impact?

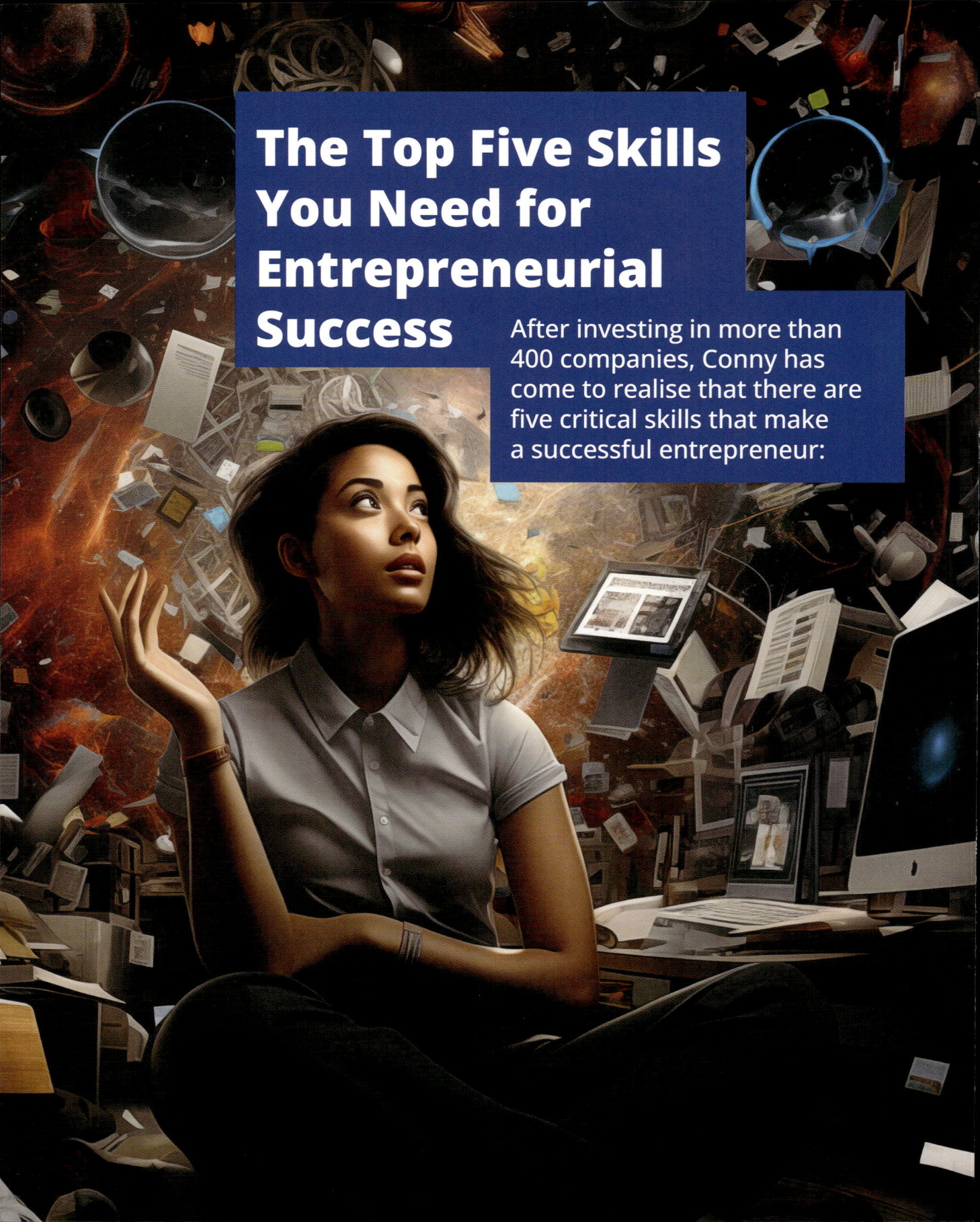

The Top Five Skills You Need for Entrepreneurial Success

After investing in more than 400 companies, Conny has come to realise that there are five critical skills that make a successful entrepreneur:

1 Ambition

"Tomorrow's leaders not only have dreams, goals, and plans. They are willing to work hard and take responsibility for turning their plans into energy, perspiration, and effort. They don't sit back and wait for someone else to turn their dreams into action."

— Denis Waitley

Having a strong drive - the idea that "I want to win" - will mobilise the unlimited energy you have inside you. Keep your eyes on the ball and always try another door when the one you are pushing doesn't open. We are often educated to think small, so beware of falling victim to such limited thinking, and instead, dream big!

Mikhail Kokorich, the founder of Destinus (a company that develops hydrogen-powered hyperplanes), is the perfect example of a brilliant entrepreneur who never fears thinking big. Not only did he build one unicorn company, which is already a major accomplishment, but through Destinus, he is building a second one!

Another example of a fearless entrepreneur is Julian Teicke, the founder of wefox, who turned down several offers to sell his company for hundreds of millions, having the confidence and ambition to build a multi-billion-dollar company by himself. Which he absolutely did.

2 Impactful communication

"Communication is a skill that you can learn. It's like riding a bicycle or typing. If you're willing to work at it, you can rapidly improve the quality of every part of your life."

— Brian Tracy

It is rare to meet a successful entrepreneur who is not also a skilled communicator. Some would say it's charisma, while others would claim it's a combination of excellent listening skills coupled with the ability to influence. I believe there is no single recipe; instead, you need to discover what style works for you and always seek to adapt it to your audience.

3 Sales mastery

"Nothing happens until someone sells something."

— Henry Ford

Communication skills alone are not enough; the ability to sell your vision, ideas, and product or service is essential to becoming a successful entrepreneur. If you don't have anyone on your team with sales and/or negotiation skills, it will be very difficult to succeed. Every start-up needs the "car-dealer" type of person. That could either be you, your business partner, or a member of your company board.

4 Resilience

"Success is not final; failure is not fatal: it is the courage to continue that counts."

— Winston S. Churchill

You already understand the value of risk-taking. With risk, however, often comes failure. There is no entrepreneur who experiences success 100 per cent of the time. Success and failure go hand in hand. Therefore, the problem is not the failure itself, but instead what you do with the information you learned from the experience and how you bounce back.

Being able to recover from setbacks without quitting, and continuing until you get the results you want, is key. Many people stop too early, most likely due to family pressure or a lack of confidence. Tech launches and new business trends take longer to succeed than most people expect, so it's easy to let slow results lead to self-doubt or giving up.

Constant problems can become discouraging, until you begin to realise that the obstacles are a normal part of the journey. Lawrence Leuschner, CEO and Co-Founder of TIER Mobility, believes it is critical to become comfortable with this constant pressure: "As an entrepreneur, you have daily challenges. You wake up on five out of seven days a week facing problems. You become experienced in facing challenges and making decisions. When you do this for a long time, you get used to it - you don't get scared, and you don't feel uncomfortable in a situation where you're under pressure. It's a bit like a football player who has practised dribbling the ball for over 10,000 hours so they can perform under pressure on game day. Over time, you will realise it's just continuous learning. Particularly when you are building a fast-growing company, you are consistently developing skills that help you grow with the challenges over time. It's a never-ending learning curve."

5 Passion

"Entrepreneurship is about doing something - to innovate and make things better . . . and at the end, it's not only about the company itself but becoming an even better society."

— Daniel Krauss

It doesn't matter how insignificant your product or business may seem to others - it is your passion that will give you the energy to win, as well as attract partners, employees, and investors. Not everybody is born to be an entrepreneur. And when someone is making a pitch, it's easy to see within minutes whether or not that person has the passion that makes their idea worth considering. Entrepreneurs who say they want to become rich are the ones to be wary of, because the purpose of an entrepreneur's life is not just about money. Instead, money is the by-product. The true purpose is to create a product or a service that will make your customers' lives better! If you put passion and effort behind that purpose, the money will come.

Conny loves starting and building companies. He loves connecting with people. Someone asked him how much time he took off when he returned from a holiday with his family. It was then that he realised that he had worked almost every day because he enjoyed it so much. It was never a chore - it was fun. Force him to do nothing for a week, and he will definitely not feel at his best. After a coaching session with a client, Crina feels uplifted and re-energised. And Dorina is tireless when it comes to testing and introducing people to the latest biohacking tools, mindfulness techniques, and personal growth. Don't get us wrong: we are firm believers in switching off and recharging. At the same time, when you follow your passion and choose your projects carefully, work is never a burden.

Reflection Questions:

- Which of these five skills do you currently possess?

- What action could you take today to improve one of these skills?

Now that we have explored the pros and cons of entrepreneurship, as well as the five skills successful entrepreneurs share, it's equally important to talk about failure - a topic people tend to avoid, but one that is critical to address in order to reach your full potential in the entrepreneurial world.

Fear of failure drives us to live safe, small lives. While we may enjoy the security of the known and the predictability of our income, hours of work and results, expecting every business idea to be a "win" cannot be part of your mindset as an entrepreneur. Limiting yourself because you fear failure as an entrepreneur is like being the captain of a ship who never leaves the harbour. All great entrepreneurs agree that taking risks and failing are a necessity:

"Evolution has only one tool, and that is failure!
Failure is a strategy to success."

— Thomas Hessler, co-founder of Zanox, UFOstart, and investor in over 200 start-ups

"Failures are part of the game. There is nothing
in the world where there is no failure.
Failures are good if you learn from them.
And don't do i t again."

— Herbert Weirather, aerospace engineer and founder of Jedsy

"Failure is just like the nature of entrepreneurship.
In a successful business, it's a chain of the failures
that finally leads to success."

— Mikhail Kokorich, CEO and founder of Destinus, Momentus Space and Astro Digital

"If things are not failing,
you are not innovating enough."

— Elon Musk

Yes, you will need to get used to "failing" if you want to become a successful entrepreneur! We would even invite you to exclude the word "failure" from your vocabulary and view everything that happens as a learning experience. Some of your actions will not lead to the results you want, but the only thing you need to do in those moments is learn from them and move on.

Lawrence Leuschner knows that even if you have already built a unicorn company, there will still be times when you are not successful, and you must be prepared for that. If you develop yourself, face challenges and grow, there is absolutely nothing that can stop you. As Lawrence puts it, "Growing, rising with your own personality and your character from the experience you accumulate - I think this is the one thing that excites me the most. And that's why I keep going, and I can't imagine stopping at any time. Maybe I will serve more in the future and work less, but I'm definitely going to continue working on my entrepreneurial journeys and adventures."

Learning from Failure

Here are just a few lessons we've learned in the face of failure. Picking ourselves up from failure, learning from the experience, and then applying that learning to future projects was the key to our successes - in business and life in general.

- **Stay committed to your long-term vision:** Once you've decided what you want to achieve, let that be your North Star in challenging times.

- **Listen to your intuition:** Remember the times when your gut was telling you something different from what your logical mind decided, and you regretted not following your intuition.

- **Be open to advice from experienced mentors:** This can be a challenging yet humbling experience. Wise guidance from those entrepreneurs who succeeded in your field can offer you insights you won't find elsewhere. They can help you avoid some of the pitfalls they experienced, thereby catapulting you to success more quickly.

- **Avoid superficial assessments** of business opportunities. Look closely at each opportunity, especially when it's a well-known industry where you are in your comfort zone.

- **Be confident!** This goes back to the fear of failure; take bigger risks and trust your instincts more. Remember these words from Conny: "In the course of your life, a train of gold will pass by five times. I've already missed three of mine, so I will take that leap of faith when I see the next one coming!"

- **Don't give up too soon.** Once again, if you're ready to sell your company because you are losing confidence that you will succeed, take a moment to pause and reflect. You may be selling just before the next big breakthrough.

- **Stay focused** and drop the business tasks that aren't aligned with your goal.

- **Get comfortable with saying no.** This is difficult for many people, but when you say yes to everything (and try to please everyone), you will end up disappointing everyone. What is worse, you will tend to let yourself down in the process as well.

This fear of failure is not your fault. It has become the norm to value security and predictability over living the life of your dreams. So many of us were brought up to "play it safe" and be "realistic" in our goals and desires. With this in mind, taking risks when success is not guaranteed can strike fear into us.

Reflection Questions:

- What lessons did you learn from your failures?

- What is your greatest business fear - and how does it relate to failure?

- What action could you take today to overcome that fear?

- What would you do if you knew you could not fail?

Embracing Risk

There is a need for radical change regarding what society values, what politicians decide, what authorities implement, and what we believe as individuals. We must stop expecting something to go wrong; stop wanting to make quick, safe money. When you take big risks and look for long-term gains, you impact not only your business but society as a whole. Fortune favours the bold!

To be bold, it is imperative to stop focusing on the shortage of resources, worrying about challenges, and concentrating solely on today's income. Be brave, and do not limit yourself when deciding where you want to take your business in three, five, or ten years.

"I think it is often easier to make progress on mega-ambitious dreams. Since no one else is crazy enough to do it, you have little competition."

— Larry Page

As an entrepreneur, the more comfortable you become with risk, the further you will go - and ultimately achieve the financial security other people only dream about.

The attitude of most European investors today.

Daniel Krauss states: *"I think that every entrepreneur is at a certain point a risk-taker just like me. They want to change things and they're not averse to taking risks. It's not only that I want mobility and green buses to be the legacy for future generations. What drives me as well is that people may learn from things we did, from how I made decisions."*

As entrepreneurs, we need to learn from the best and always look forward, asking ourselves, "Is this a market that will grow in the future?" The truth is that many "safe" jobs - those in traditional industries like banking and steel - will not even exist in their current form over time. Instead of investing in the products we have now, we should move on towards new technologies, such as artificial intelligence, augmented reality, renewable energy, biotechnology, telemedicine, fintech, or cybersecurity, to name just a few.

Europeans' appetite for risky start-ups or tech investments is still relatively low, so they prefer to invest in real estate and traditional industries with little risk. In retrospect, we can see that this strategy was the wrong decision. A single tech company such as Apple is now worth more than all the stock-listed companies in Germany combined.

Conny has a great example from when he visited Amazon in 2000:

> # If we aren't willing to take a gamble, how will we ever progress beyond the status quo?

"When I returned home, I was so excited about the company and shared with all the investors in my network the great potential it had. Not only did they not trust me or invest, but whenever they heard any bad news about Amazon, those investors relentlessly reminded me, 'Isn't that the company you wanted to invest in?' and 'They're still not making money; they'll go bust; they'll disappear.' Today, more than 50 per cent of the worldwide e-commerce market is in the hands of Amazon. Amazon is worth more than all German, Swiss, and Austrian companies with a stock listing, combined. It's a huge success story, isn't it? There is a difference between gaining market share and increasing the valuation of a company and profitability. In Europe, we only discuss profitability, but we don't share a vision that you will become the absolute leader in a huge market which does not exist at the moment. What I'm talking about is a completely different mindset - a truly winning one!"

This example illustrates the dire need for more courageous entrepreneurs, investors, and politicians who make brave decisions and are willing to take risks - and even fail. Let's say that we decide, as a society, to move toward hydrogen fuel. In doing so, we are making a bet despite previous experience. But if we aren't willing to take a stand and take a gamble, how will we ever progress beyond the status quo?

We also need to shift from the destructive money mindset we have. If somebody is wealthy, the first thing that often comes to mind for many people is that the person must have gotten exceedingly lucky or done something shady or illegal to get there. With that kind of mental construct, how can we expect our children to become financially independent? What's more, if you fail in Europe, go bankrupt, or are accused of wrongdoing, you will be attacked so mercilessly that it's next to impossible to get a second chance. When someone fails in the U.S., for example, people say, "Wow! At least he tried! Let's see how he comes back."

Only when each of us starts accepting failures as being a necessary part of the learning process will we have more "lighthouse entrepreneurs" and a more powerful start-up ecosystem.

The wrong approach to risk.

Bringing Your Dreams to Life: What Are Your Goals?

Now is the moment of truth: get ready to consider what you believe is possible for your business. It is important to translate what you're doing into measurable metrics and keep alive your passion for adding value through everything you do. That will carry you to the finish line.

"For those who think business exists to make a profit, I suggest they think again. Business makes a profit to exist. Surely it must exist for some higher, nobler purpose than that."

— Ray Anderson

The only way to achieve your goals is to have solid beliefs supporting you. Notice how Conny's beliefs evolved over time: "I used to call myself an 'opportunistic bargain hunter.' In other words, I was great at spotting start-ups which required minimum investment. As a result, I only pursued opportunities that led to small, incremental business growth. I used to believe that if I invested large amounts of money, I would put myself and my family at too much risk."

Holding onto these beliefs would have prevented Conny from starting a billion-dollar project like the SPAC. Once he realised those beliefs were limiting his potential, Conny accepted that he could feel safe while executing bigger investments.

An unshakable belief in yourself and your business potential is key. Walid Abboud, serial entrepreneur and investor, for example, remembers how his first investors laughed when he brought in his first two partners—and when he told them they should expect a US$1 million turnover in the first year. Not only did that happen, but within ten years, his successful pharmaceutical distribution business was making US$1 million per day. What is essential in his story is his belief that "work is not sacrifice. Of course, there are parts of my work I don't enjoy, and I am finding ways to delegate or outsource those parts. Business for me now is like a game, a constant mental stimulation." Take some time to get clear on the goals you have for your business, envisioning what you can achieve.

Reflection Questions:

- What is the most ambitious goal you have for your company?

- How will your abilities make your business a success?

- What opportunities are available for your business?

Notice which beliefs may be limiting you. Do you want to hold onto them? Look at yourself and the world through a "possibility" lens.

Reflection Questions:

- Which beliefs are limiting you?

- What would be the powerful beliefs to catapult you towards achieving your goals?

LET'S REVIEW

In this chapter, we have discussed how exciting it can be to live the life of an entrepreneur, and have shared some valuable insights on entrepreneurship. At the same time, we made you aware of the pros and cons of entrepreneurship, as well as five skills that are necessary to becoming a successful entrepreneur.

While many people only want to look at the glamorous aspects of entrepreneurship, it is important to be aware of the obstacles that may stand in your way. By remembering that taking risks and facing challenges - including failure - are a necessary component of the journey, you can stay focused on your goals and the beliefs, experiences, and actions that will help make success a reality!

As Conny is fond of saying, "*You might have sleepless nights, but I could not think of anything more rewarding than being a successful entrepreneur. Even though at first it may look more risky than working as an employee, I believe when all is said and done, it is less risky. Regardless of whether you fail or succeed with your first ventures, you will learn a valuable set of skills that allow you to start a new venture anytime. And one day, looking back, you will realise it was worth it.*"

WHAT'S NEXT

Of course, entrepreneurial success requires significant energy and drive, so the next chapter will help you clarify your purpose and address why it is so crucial to maintain a single-minded focus to achieve your goals. With a clear vision, you can withstand the pressures of entrepreneurship, as your sense of purpose will help guide your actions and decision-making.

"You can only become
truly accomplished
at something you love.
Don't make money your goal.
Instead, pursue the things
you love doing
and then do them so well
that people can't take
their eyes off of you."

— Maya Angelou

CHAPTER TWO

Know Your "Why":
Do It with Purpose

"It all starts with WHY. By WHY I mean, what is your purpose, cause or belief? WHY does your company exist? WHY do you get out of bed every morning? And WHY should anyone care?"

— Simon Sinek

FROM MONEY TO PURPOSE:

How My First Business Venture Helped Me Discover Both

When I started my entrepreneurial journey forty years ago at a flea market, I had no higher purpose; I just wanted to make money to buy things. With my first company, SABECO - which developed an emergency health card to allow basic data to be provided to emergency doctors - I understood for the first time the impact my business might have on the world. But it wasn't until I put a microchip in this plastic card and started ACG - my first unicorn company - that my journey towards finding my purpose began . . .

At the time, we were facing competition from an old, established, slow-moving giant in the smart-card industry, and they were doing everything they could to keep other people out of the market. Our purpose became this: democratise and diversify the industry, offering better products at lower prices. All of us at the company felt like Robin Hood, challenging the Sheriff of Nottingham. Just as Robin Hood ran through Sherwood Forest, stealing from the rich to benefit the poor, we felt as if we were doing a similar service for people who couldn't afford our competitor's pricey product. So, whenever they came into "our forest," we tried to take some business from them. We felt like we were fighting for justice!

Even though our offices were not as fancy, and our travel budgets were far more limited, the joy came from our higher purpose: that incredible feeling of being together on a joint mission to do good in the world. When recruiting people, we would actually ask them, "Do you want to work for the Sheriff of Nottingham . . . or come over to the 'good' side?"

Suddenly, I became the driver of an entire industry, and my vision expanded to developing the best and most affordable smart cards available on the market - to make people's lives safer and more convenient. Propelled by this vision of limitless opportunities, the business expanded like nothing I had ever witnessed before, surging from one to 340 million Euros in sales, in a mere three years' time.

After I sold ACG, I became financially independent and decided I wanted to become the biggest networker in the world. My purpose was growing, evolving, and changing yet again. Knowing that it's impossible to expand a network with only one-on-one meetings. Today, as one of the most active start-up investors in Europe, my purpose is to help young entrepreneurs overcome the challenges of starting a business and guide them to fruitful outcomes. I also enjoy sharing my knowledge and being a sounding board for successful entrepreneurs.

Having lived the roles of serial entrepreneur, political advisor, and start-up investor to the fullest, I learned that your purpose and vision may change over the years. And I learned that by partnering with like-minded people, you can achieve much more than on your own. Currently, sharing with Crina and Dorina the vision to impact entrepreneurs around the world, by offering opportunities for self-development, learning, and growth, brought this book to life.

— Conny

WHY ARE WE HERE?

"The two most important days in life are the day you are born and the day you discover the reason why."

— Mark Twain

It might take a long time to realise what your purpose is. Not knowing it in the beginning is rather typical for entrepreneurs, though. Think about it: how many people take the time to ask themselves,

Reflection Questions:

- Why do I wake up in the morning?

- What would I love to do? What am I here to create?

We are not taught how to find our purpose in school, and we don't always give ourselves the gift of time and reflection to discover it. Not only that, but your purpose may grow and

Your purpose may grow and evolve in time.

evolve throughout your life, as ours did, so it may take several attempts to find it. However, if you're reading this chapter and wondering what your purpose might be, you're in the right place. Helping you find it is exactly what this chapter is for!

If you're reading this book, you most likely have a strong desire to grow, learn, become a better version of yourself every single day . . . and ultimately, leave a legacy. In order to achieve these goals, it is important to take time to explore your purpose - the reason for your existence - as well as the impact you want to make on the world.

The rewards of discovering your true purpose are great. Once you find that purpose, you will have discovered your North Star, which will always guide your life and business in the right direction. Whenever confronted with a challenge or question, simply remember your purpose, and the answers will be much easier to find.

Purpose is something very personal. There is no right or wrong. Don't compare yours with anyone else's purpose. For some, their purpose may be to innovate and create new products, while others want to raise happy children and be of service. A firefighter's purpose might be to save lives, a policeman's purpose could be to help people feel safe, and a teacher's to prepare the next generation to become contributing citizens in society. The best politicians might want to make their community, city, or country better - and have a positive impact on society.

Why Is It Important to Have a Purpose?

"If you don't know where you are going, every road will get you nowhere."

— Henry Kissinger

Before we continue any further, let us explore why finding your purpose is worth the time investment. First, it is extremely difficult to become successful without a purpose - and without purpose, it is difficult to enjoy a happy, fulfilled life.

A clear purpose also becomes your compass. It helps you define your vision, create your game plan, set priorities, and learn to say no at the right time. It helps you navigate life and business through uncertainty.

A clear purpose is "the hidden secret" to create a fulfilling life, giving you the energy to manage even the toughest days.

Michael Hengl, CEO of 1492 - a think tank focused on enhancing the collective intelligence of organisations, teams, and ecosystems - shares how his life was transformed when he aligned with his purpose: "By finding my passion, my vocation, and being obsessed with one thing, all my decisions became easier. Instead of feeling I sacrifice a lot, regretting the things I was saying no to, I had a very liberating feeling. A sense of freedom I can only recommend."

Navigating between her work as an author, activist, coach, and mentor for both Hay House writers and her PR business, Jessica Huie believes that, as long as you devote yourself to growing and staying in integrity with the values of goodness and service, your purpose will actually find you! "My greatest intention is to become more of who I'm here to be - and to lose that which I'm not, which is all the stuff that we acquire as we go through life: all the baggage, unhelpful ego wrangling, overthinking, insecurity, comparison, impostor syndrome, and all the things that stop us from allowing the essence of who we are to shine and touch others." By transcending her ego, Jessica believes that she can stop trying to control everything and instead embrace whatever life allows.

When we interviewed Jessica for this book, she expanded on the importance of having a purpose in life: "Purpose is the very foundation for me. It's the fuel that motivates me to take action, particularly when my head tells me I'd rather not. It's the very thing that drives me onward, through the inevitable challenges that come with running a business and putting yourself out there, stepping out of your comfort zone, allowing yourself to be seen, with all of the vulnerability that comes with that, and just showing up. Purpose is both the fuel and the reason. It's bigger than myself. And that connects me to life. It connects me to others. It connects me to my tiny but crucial role in the broader scheme of things."

"Let your why form the foundation of your enterprise and your cause - and its meaning will keep your ship afloat through rough seas. This will enable you to smile at your reflection each morning, content in the knowledge that your worthiness stems not from the car you drive nor your bank balance, but from who you are."

— Jessica Huie

Quite often, the way to discover your purpose is totally unexpected — and less joyful than the picture a Hollywood movie would paint. When he set a Guinness World Record by crossing the Antarctic to the Southern Pole of Inaccessibility in 2006, Henry Cookson - explorer and founder of Cookson Adventures - just wanted to do something interesting and different. By no means was he attempting to receive recognition for his venture. Instead, Henry shared: "I was unhappy. I knew I had talents and abilities, but I felt discomfort in selling something I did not believe in . . . and I wasn't aware of something I could believe in. I spent time at an investment bank and felt I wasn't being honest. I was struggling where my place in the world was, where could I put my talents, education, charms, things I knew I had deep down. I was genuinely miserable at home, and my family situation wasn't great. The trip felt like a big runaway, like an escape! But that gave me motivation. Thankfully, through the camaraderie of being with two very good friends, going into extraordinary parts of the planet, and achieving huge feats of endurance, I started seeing the world differently."

After fifty-five days and a 1,700-kilometre kite ski trip to the centre of Antarctica, being out of range of aircraft pickup and going through areas that no human ever laid eyes on, Henry returned to London where his family was in pieces. He had no money and no prospects for the future, but he realised that he had found his purpose: "I want to make this my life, but I want to do it authentically. There were two routes I could take: become a professional explorer with the chest beating and telling everyone what I've done, writing books and giving interviews, which sort of means you have to tell some stories and exaggerate, or alternatively, become a humble guide. For me, it was becoming the humble guide. It was not even a consideration. I got approached by several production companies to go on television and everything else. But again, I see television as performance; it's not real, and I felt I have to tell the truth, the real story. And that has always been the case in terms of what we do, in my business. There are no exaggerations, no silly claims. This is what we've done and who we are - very impressive, incredible staff, but we don't lie. And this probably held back the business a bit."

These are the values on which one of the most exclusive travel companies of our time was built. Described by the *Financial Times* as "a 2.0 version of the traditional fearless British explorer," Henry Cookson and his team of experts have guided the Walking with the Wounded charity expedition to the North Pole with HRH Prince Harry, rehomed giant tortoises by helicopter, scaled volcanos in Nicaragua, and discovered a new-

Without purpose what are we? Just success and material possessions I don't think is going to make you happy alone.

species of orca. "Without purpose what are we? Just success and material possessions I don't think is going to make you happy alone." Over time, Henry's life purpose has evolved towards "sharing what I've seen and my knowledge with the people who are shaping the world, those who are looked up to, the opinion makers, so they make financial decisions to change the world for the good of future generations. If I can help them see and understand what I've seen, just by one fraction, that leveraged with the power they have, is millions of times more impactful than what I could ever do as an individual.

"My hope is to be a catalyst, showing people the breathtaking beauty and the issues out there, so they appreciate what nature is. These are highly functioning, capable people. And they've been working nonstop to achieve their substantial goals. Maybe within that, they haven't had the time to stop and appreciate what nature really is. I am good at fixing things. I'm good at making solutions. I've done some crazy things in the past to achieve almost impossible goals in our trips. We need the highly successful entrepreneurs to now put their energies into the reality of our world and what that means for their children and their grandchildren. So, if I can touch these people and affect them, even in a small fraction, then I'm succeeding, and my purpose is being fulfilled."

Having travelled across the world and volunteered in Costa Rica, India, and Indonesia, Lila Behr, ecopreneur and founder of Gaia Protection, already knows that her purpose is to "discover, promote, and inspire innovative solutions that can shape resilient communities for the future. I envision a world where our children and future generations can reach their full potential, while enjoying every moment of life they are given."

Lila's vision rests upon three pillars: "awaken, heal, and love," representing her personal journey and the collective transformation essential for creating resilient communities. First, she highlights the importance of healing at a personal level by getting adequate rest, taking breaks, and detaching from technology - as well as nurturing positive thoughts and forging meaningful connections with others. From there, healing efforts can extend into communities and the environment through retreats, workshops, or seminars to promote collective healing.

When it comes to love, "the foundation of all progress in our world," as Lila describes it, she rightly says that "without love, purpose can quickly lose its significance. Finding something we genuinely enjoy gives us a reason to wake up each morning. Personally, I find profound joy in dance and music, aspiring for moments where my children and family can share these passions."

Finding Your Purpose Using the IKIGAI Method

If you're not entirely clear on your purpose yet, there is an excellent structured approach that can help you discover it: Ikigai.

生き甲斐

ikigai

[ee-kee-gahy] Japanese

"A reason for being" the thing that gets you up in the morning. Having a sense of purpose in life and a feeling of well-being.

IKIGAI is the Japanese method for examining "what life is worth living for." The term comes from the combination of two words: "iki" (which means life / being alive) and "gai" (meaning effect/result). IKIGAI helps you summarise the reason you have for being alive. As Hector Garcia and Francesc Miralles mentioned in their book Ikigai: The Japanese Secret to a Long and Happy Life, this philosophy began more than 1,000 years ago and was translated into "the happiness of always being busy." which led to the Okinawa Island having the highest percentage of centenarians in the world.

In Conny's words, "I was very grateful to work on my IKIGAI with Ralph Höfliger as my coach, who challenged me to find my real purpose - why I get up in the morning. It was a game-changer. I got to look back and reflect on what I wanted to do with the second half of my life. In the end, what do I burn for? I spent weeks thinking about this and I kept coming back to it because I never questioned what I truly love in my life before. I never listed what I am good at. I never asked myself: what does the world truly need from me? Lastly, I never put these together to help answer the compelling question of what I get paid for.

---

1 - IKIGAI - Oliver, Laura, "Is this Japanese concept the secret to a long, happy, meaningful life?" World Economic Forum, August 9, 2017, https://www.weforum.org/agenda/2017/08/is-this-japanese-concept-the-secret-to-a-long-life/.

CHAPTER TWO

"For me, most interesting was the interrelation between these four questions, and the clear, visual, life blueprint you get on one page. You might find that many of the questions in the IKIGAI are already in your head. However, finding your purpose might require a few iterations and someone to challenge you, asking the right questions to guide your reflections in a powerful, structured way. In addition, remember that your Ikigai is dynamic, changing continuously over time as both you and the world around you evolve.

"When was the last time you asked yourself those questions? Do you sometimes lie in bed before you fall asleep and think about these things? Do you have a partner with whom you can discuss such important topics?

"I had a few major discoveries during my IKIGAI journey. I realised that I don't commit enough time to the things I really love. I then asked myself if I needed to set different priorities. Reflecting on what I am good at, I also realised what my weaknesses are.

"Throughout my life, I focused on areas I excel in, but in order to maximise your strengths, it's important to know and be comfortable with your weaknesses. It was also interesting to ask others for input during this process, as it gave me a better understanding of what people appreciate about me and what I want to improve.

Why do I get up in the morning? What do I really burn for?

"The IKIGAI gave me the answers to the questions 'Why do I get up in the morning?' and 'What do I really burn for?' The answers lie at the centre of the model, my purpose. In my case, I found that I am a born networker looking for the 'golden treasure' - the start-ups that really make the difference. One thing I realised while doing my Ikigai was that the world still needs people with networking capabilities. I found out very early that I am a networker. I have the skills, love meeting people, and the world is longing for networking opportunities. I just hadn't found a way to get paid for it. I discovered in my journey, however, that 'connecting the right people' came up frequently. Perhaps this is the core of my existence. Doing my IKIGAI also made me realise that I am addicted to happiness. For me, happiness is the ultimate reason and the main purpose for which we are on earth. And that time is precious - I only have one life!"

When you're ready, start by exploring: **"What you are GOOD at?"**

Ask yourself: "What am I good at? What am I proud of." Write down whatever comes to your mind in the left semicircle. If you find yourself challenged by the questions, start considering what other people might appreciate about you at work. Ask yourself, "When I got positive feedback from others, what were they saying I was good at? When were others particularly impressed by what I did?"

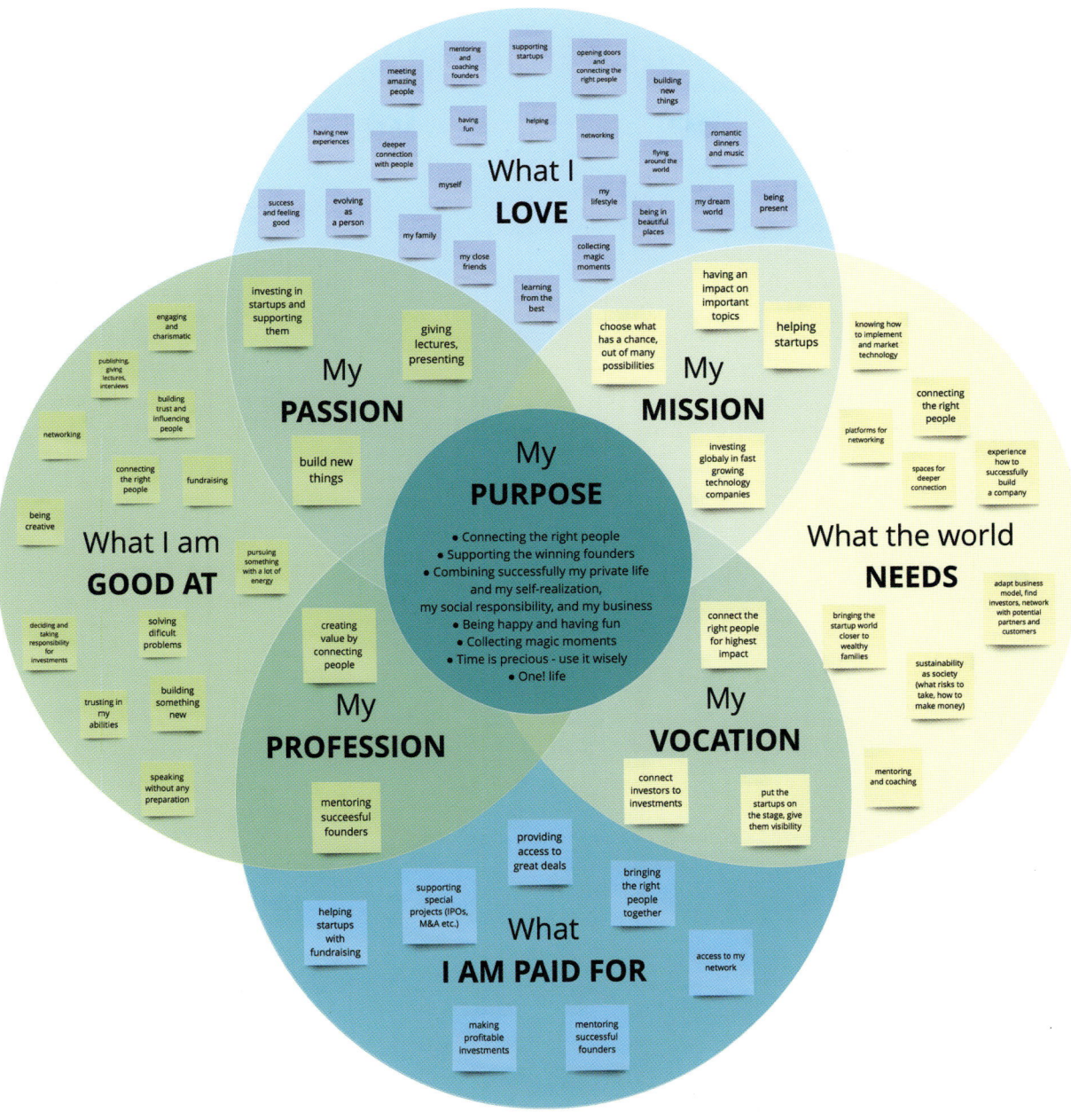

What I
LOVE

mentoring and coaching founders
supporting startups
opening doors and connecting the right people
meeting amazing people
building new things
having new experiences
having fun
helping
networking
deeper connection with people
flying around the world
romantic dinners and music
myself
my lifestyle
being present
success and feeling good
evolving as a person
being in beautiful places
my dream world
my family
my close friends
collecting magic moments
learning from the best

My
PASSION

investing in startups and supporting them
giving lectures, presenting
engaging and charismatic
publishing, giving lectures, interviews
building trust and influencing people
networking
build new things
connecting the right people
fundraising
being creative

My
MISSION

having an impact on important topics
helping startups
choose what has a chance, out of many possibilities
knowing how to implement and market technology
connecting the right people
platforms for networking
spaces for deeper connection
experience how to successfully build a company
investing globally in fast growing technology companies

My
PURPOSE

• Connecting the right people
• Supporting the winning founders
• Combining successfully my private life and my self-realization, my social responsibility, and my business
• Being happy and having fun
• Collecting magic moments
• Time is precious - use it wisely
• One! life

What I am
GOOD AT

pursuing something with a lot of energy
deciding and taking responsibility for investments
solving difficult problems
trusting in my abilities
building something new
speaking without any preparation
creating value by connecting people

What the world
NEEDS

adapt business model, find investors, network with potential partners and customers
bringing the startup world closer to wealthy families
connect the right people for highest impact
sustainability as society (what risks to take, how to make money)
mentoring and coaching

My
PROFESSION

mentoring succeesful founders

My
VOCATION

connect investors to investments
put the startups on the stage, give them visibility

What
I AM PAID FOR

providing access to great deals
bringing the right people together
supporting special projects (IPOs, M&A etc.)
helping startups with fundraising
access to my network
making profitable investments
mentoring successful founders

When nothing more comes to mind, move on to exploring: **"What you LOVE."** Ask yourself: "What do I really love? What brings me joy and fulfilment? What makes my heart sing?" In the upper petal, write down whatever comes to your mind. Don't limit yourself to work; list everything you truly love doing. What excites you in your free time? What are the activities you could totally lose yourself in for hours, yet feel energised when you finish the activity?

The next step is to think about: **"What the world NEEDS."** Ask yourself: "What does the world need from me?" Consider the biggest problems we are faced with and what is required to solve them. Don't think small, discounting your ability to assess the problems humanity is having now. Trust that ideas will come just from asking what contribution is needed from you, considering your skills, knowledge, and passions.

Finally, reflect on: **"What you can be PAID for."** Ask yourself: "What value can I create (or want to create in the future) for which people or organisations would be willing to pay?" Take into account both practical and creative solutions, considering the "pain" you could alleviate that someone would be willing to pay for. Now, let's dive into the steps that will guide you towards revealing your IKIGAI. Ideally, you want to align your strengths and what you love with what you're getting paid for. If you choose a job where you can't

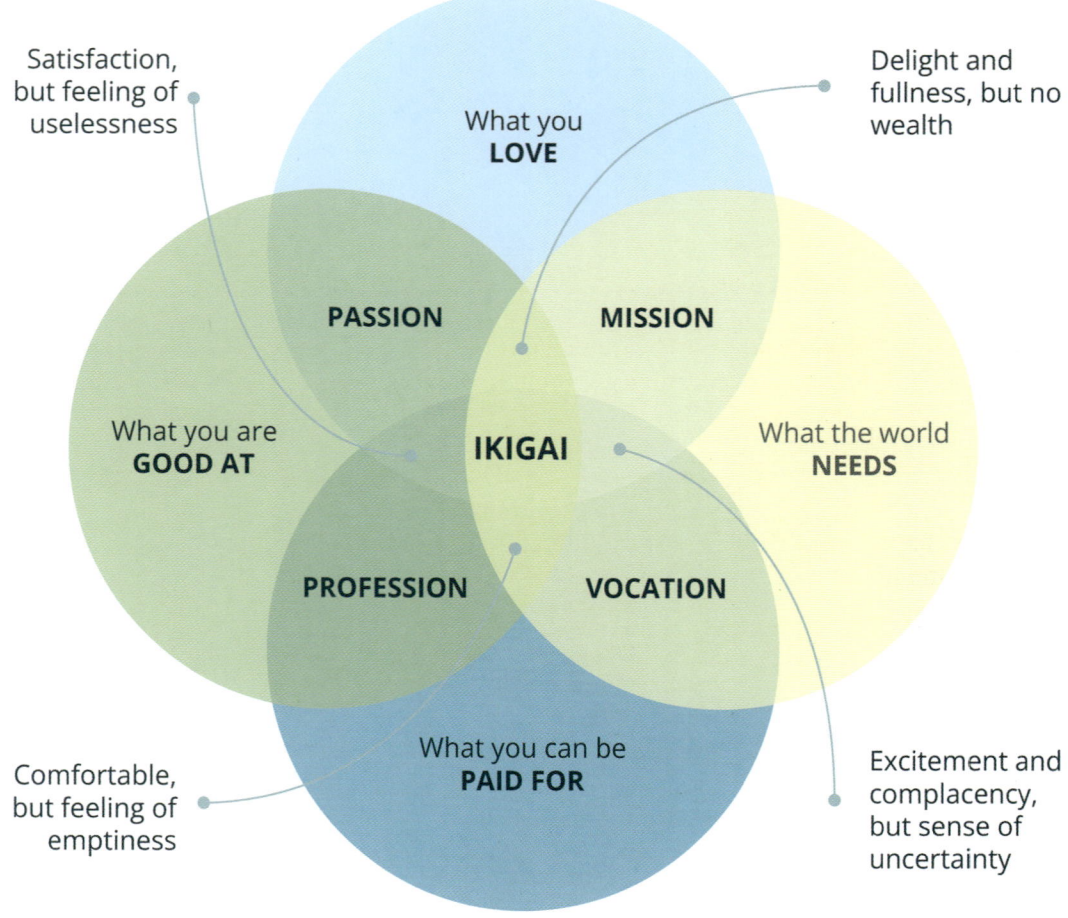

apply your talent, you're unable to give your best. By doing your IKIGAI now, you have the opportunity of an impactful reset.

Doing your IKIGAI requires your full attention, presence, and awareness. It requires an open mind and curiosity to discover new things about yourself. You must dedicate time for it - up to two hours away from distractions. Have a pen and the IKIGAI template in front of you.

Once you've finished writing all your answers, take a short break. Then, with a fresh pair of eyes, read what you have written so far on the IKIGAI diagram. Add anything that comes to mind in response to the four foundational questions.

You are now ready to integrate what you've written thus far, to uncover your passions, mission, vocation, and profession through the intersections of the circles.

- First, look at the overlap between "What you are GOOD AT" and "What you LOVE." Summarise what activity or business results from bringing together all those insights and write it down as your **passion**.
- Secondly, focus on the overlap between "What you LOVE" and "What the WORLD NEEDS" to find your **mission**.
- Third, combine "What the WORLD NEEDS" and "What you can be PAID for" to reveal, in one succinct sentence, your **vocation**.
- Finally, look at the intersection between "What you can be PAID for" and "What you are GOOD AT" to determine your **profession**.

Once again, it's time for a break. Stretch your body, take a few deep breaths, and look at the entire picture, noticing how you feel and observing the thoughts that come to your mind. If you want to add or change something, now is the time—because next, you will extract the essence, from everything you've captured, to name your life purpose: the real reason to wake up every morning energised, eager to start your day.

As life coach and IKIGAI expert Ralph Höfliger highlights, "This last step is an intuitive process, something many of us are not used to doing or trusting. It is less about thinking what you should write and more about listening to your inner voice, your intuition. Therefore, it is important that you relax and enter a state of total presence and awareness, connecting with your higher self. Then, looking at your IKIGAI in an integrative way, just ask yourself: What is my life purpose? And then listen. Be totally calm, present, and listen. Your life purpose will appear. If you are distracted by other thoughts, just let them go, like clouds passing in a clear, blue sky. Stay calm, relaxed and with a silent mind, until your life purpose appears. You will know when you have found it!"

Next Steps in the Journey

The better you know yourself, the easier it is to find your purpose. That is why we recommend doing a personality test and reflecting on the insights. There are hundreds of tests to choose from, including MBTI, Typefinder (sixteen personalities), DISC, Insights, Enneagram (nine personalities), HEXACO or the PrinciplesYou - especially designed for entrepreneurs by Ray Dalio and Adam Grant,[2] just to name a few.

---

2 - Dalio, Ray, "Principles You," https://principlesyou.com.

Level Up: From Purpose to Impact

"You can never have an impact on society if you have not changed yourself."

— Nelson Mandela

A clear purpose enables you to have an impact on the world. As an entrepreneur, it doesn't matter if you are big or small. You are a powerful creator! You have a great responsibility. You have the freedom to choose how your work and life will impact the people around you for generations to come.

So, if you have a company, it's important to share a common business purpose with your team, employees, investors, and clients.

> **As an entrepreneur, it doesn't matter if you are big or small. You are a powerful creator!**

Everyone in your company should understand it, because people united around a common purpose can achieve almost anything!

What we have observed during our careers is that the more successful you are as an entrepreneur, the more impact you want to have and the bigger your responsibility becomes. You want your work to have meaning, leaving behind something that will last long after you are gone: something bigger than just you. In the words of Jane Goodall: "You cannot get through a single day without having an impact on the world around you. What you do makes a difference, and you have to decide what kind of difference you want to make."

You might struggle with this idea if you are at the start of your journey. You might think that there is no way you can have an impact. But with everything you say or do, you impact the people around you - be it your children, your friends, or your team at work. If you're still not ready to accept this idea, think about what the Dalai Lama said: "If you think you are too small to make a difference, try sleeping with a mosquito."

Fortunately, you do not need to wait until you've accumulated a fortune to take action that makes a lasting impact. Today, more and more leaders are concerned about our environment and sustainability, so they are reflecting this in their business and organisational models. A good example of this are the Sustainable Development Goals (SDGs),[3] developed in 2015 by the UN. These goals represent the world's shared plan to end extreme poverty, reduce inequality, and protect the planet by 2030. They continue to be a source of inspiration for people across all sectors, geographies, and cultures.

Henry Cookson believes, "It is those people who make an impact on the planet in terms of our humanity and saving our home that will be remembered. Some people are very good at creating wealth and businesses and being entrepreneurs. But you could apply that entrepreneurial skill to solving

---

3 - "The Global Goals For Sustainable Development," United Nation, https://sdgs.un.org/goals#goals.

the problems of the planet. And I know it's not easy to unwind from existing commitments. So, we need to ask ourselves, what is actually meaningful? You will be another rich guy in the graveyard. And as the world becomes wealthier, with more people and an explosion of innovation caused by AI, even the great billionaires of our time are going to fall into little footnotes in history. My impact is to keep our planet safe by helping these people find their true legacy."

When asked about the impact she wants to have, Lila Behr needed no time to reflect, "I want to leave the planet in a better state than when I entered it. I aim to create a life on earth that is worth living for my children and future generations. This means envisioning a world with clean air, access to fresh drinking water, and thriving biodiversity."

As a successful entrepreneur, your ultimate goal is to impact others: your employees, your family, your community, and your industry. We want to have a long-lasting positive impact, and one way to achieve it is through sustainability. More and more investors know that companies committed to sustainability perform better. What will that mean for you? Perhaps sustainability means doing work that supports the SDG - or maybe your impact will be felt somewhere else. Regardless of your impact, please know that you have the power to affect the economy, environment, and society as a whole . . . and how exciting is that?!

It is those people who make an impact on the planet in terms of our humanity and saving our home that will be remembered.

Reflection Questions:

- What is the impact you want to have?

- What sustainability goal is your business already aligned with?

- What are you inspired to improve in the coming years?

While coaching and mentoring people, we have observed that finding a purpose becomes more and more important as you get older. It might have to do with the realisation that time is precious. If you have a purpose, it helps you become more resilient. In the end, you are never too old to find a purpose in your life. Nevertheless, we have been thrilled to see young entrepreneurs passionately driven by a clear purpose and committed to sustainability.

LET'S REVIEW

In this chapter, we established the importance of discovering your purpose in life. Not only will this increase your chances for success, but it will also serve as your North Star in both professional and personal decision-making.

We also presented a highly effective method to help you discover your purpose with IKIGAI. Without a doubt, this incredibly powerful tool can help you discover what will transform your life into one of meaning, fulfilment and make a true impact on the world.

WHAT'S NEXT

Discovering your purpose - and making an impact in the world - does not happen in a vacuum. Rather, the important people in your life play a pivotal role, which is why tending to relationships in your life is vital to your success, not just personally but also professionally. That is why the next chapter will explore the intersection between successful entrepreneurship and successful relationships.

CHAPTER THREE

Cultivate Meaningful Connections:
The Power of Human Relations and Networking

"The meeting of two personalities is like the contact of two chemical substances: if there is any reaction, both are transformed."

— Carl Jung

JOURNEYS OF THE HEART:
Discovering Life's Richness through Unexpected Friendships

The first time I realised the power of relationships was when I listened to the words of motivational speaker Denis Waitley. He emphasised the life-changing aspects of networking and relationships - and showed me how cultivating meaningful connections can transform your world. Soon after this, I was fortunate enough to encounter one of these life-changing relationships during a talk show . . .

In 1999, I was invited to appear on a German talk show, where I met a young politician named Guido Westerwelle. Right from the beginning, we liked each other very much. At that time, he was serving as secretary-general of the Free Democratic Party (FDP) in Germany, but he had even bigger ambitions. Although we rarely shared the same political opinions, we enjoyed our conversations and started spending more and more time together.

As a successful entrepreneur, my focus was to advise him on economic topics and international politics. In time, I became responsible for organising the election campaigns and financing for the FDP. Shortly after I assumed these responsibilities, Guido became the president of the Liberal Party and then, in 2009, the foreign minister and vice-chancellor of Germany. As I spent more time in Berlin and travelled with Guido to various countries all over the world, our connection deepened further, and we developed great trust in each other.

One interesting aspect of our relationship was that Guido was gay (and I am not). During that time, people were still extremely critical of anyone who was not heterosexual - and gay politicians were practically non-existent, except for the Mayor of Berlin, Claus Wowereit. Incidentally, Wowereit was the individual who coined the phrase, "Berlin is poor . . . but sexy!"

As I travelled with Guido, we faced an ongoing challenge: some of the wealthiest families and most influential people would not agree to meet the vice-chancellor because he was gay. But that was not the only challenge. For example, during an official visit to China, all local gay bars and clubs were coincidentally investigated the moment we landed with the German Airforce. It was hard for Guido not to take it personally. What I found amusing was that everyone then became convinced that I was also gay - a completely new experience for me!

Surprisingly, we sometimes found much more kind and accepting politicians in the most unexpected places - like several leaders of Arabian countries. When I met the king of Saudi Arabia for the first time, I was accompanying Guido on one of his first trips to the country. Upon our arrival, the king welcomed us personally and showed Guido several paintings in his palace. Guido truly appreciated the paintings, and his enthusiasm was contagious. He would exclaim, "OMG, this is amazing! How breathtaking!" So much that the king actually felt obliged to offer (and deliver) all those paintings immediately to the aircraft. Witnessing the power of human connection in this way, I understood on a profound level how important awareness and acceptance of human differences are in the world.

Of all the politicians I have ever met in my life, Guido was by far the most amazing character. He could be tough when times called for it, and at other times, he displayed extraordinary empathy and sensitivity.

In 2016, Guido tragically lost his battle to cancer. His diagnosis was a shock for me. His determination to fight leukaemia was incredible, demonstrating his strength of character. One of the most difficult moments of my life was helping to carry Guido`s coffin. We were followed by lots of cameras, and I shed many tears that day. Guido's death made me painfully aware of the importance of health - because everything else is irrelevant if you don't have that.

Guido taught me many important life lessons. For instance, when America, England, and France attacked Libya (in order to teach Gaddafi a lesson), there was immense international pressure on Guido for Germany to join this alliance. He decided to stay neutral, along with countries like Russia, China, India, and Brazil. Initially, I felt so embarrassed about this decision; in fact, we got into our first serious fight over this issue. Even his bodyguards started to worry.

Many years later, I realised that his choice was probably one of the smartest decisions a German politician could have made in decades. Before the attack, Libya was not perfect, but generally a prosperous, safe country. Now, it is a fallen state, ruled by warlords. Through this experience, I learned that you must think through a situation from the beginning to the end, considering all potential implications. And, if you take something (or someone) out, you also need a good plan to replace it - which applies to all situations in life.

Some of my most memorable evenings with Guido involved lengthy political discussions at my home in Mallorca. These helped me realise that, even when it comes to a topic you may think you know everything about, there will be someone who can teach you more! In other words, "any master can find their master"!

The friendship I was fortunate to have with Guido Westerwelle is a constant reminder that a deep human connection transcends societal norms, overcomes differences of opinions, and has a lifelong transformative power.

— Conny

LAYERS OF CONNECTION:
Nurturing Success through Relationships

"A deep sense of love and belonging is an irreducible need of all people. We are biologically, cognitively, physically, and spiritually wired to love, to be loved, and to belong. When those needs are not met, we don't function as we were meant to. We break. We fall apart. We numb. We ache. We hurt others. We get sick... The absence of love and belonging will always lead to suffering."

— Brené Brown

To live a fulfilling life, it is crucial to dedicate time to your relationships and reflect on the way you connect with people. Why are our relationships so important? Because, as the Dalai Lama brilliantly noted, "We human beings are social beings. We come into the world as the result of others' actions. We survive here in dependence on others. Whether we like it or not, there is hardly a moment of our lives when we do not benefit from others' activities. For this reason, it is hardly surprising that most of our happiness arises in the context of our relationships with others."

...we must get our relationships right to thrive.

While we might not need deep connections with people to survive, when it comes to "success" in business or as a member of society, we thrive only when we get our relationships right. From the

CHAPTER THREE

relationships we build at work with partners, teams, potential investors, and clients, to the family relationships we have with parents, siblings, children, life partners, or friends, human connections often serve as our source of energy and motivation to drive us forward - as well as the solid rock we rely on to build business success.

Conny encourages us to imagine relationships like an onion: the centre represents the people you would die for, such as your children, the love of your life, or your spouse. The next layer consists of those you trust with your heart and who have been with you during good and bad times. These are the special people who know what you're thinking, even before you've said a word - your close friends and family. After that come your business partners and extended circle of friends.

For Conny, this is a particularly special circle, since he tends to view team members as friends and family. The next layer represents your business network, as well as all the people you admire and remain connected with.

The First Layer: Family & Loved Ones

"I am convinced that material things can contribute a lot to making one's life pleasant, but, basically, if you do not have very good friends and relatives who matter to you, life will be really empty and sad and material things cease to be important."

— David Rockefeller

Who would be in the centre of your onion? Calling these people to mind, consider how much time, attention, and energy you give to these special people. Think about how you communicate your gratitude toward them, through your words and actions. Imagine how they would react, if you told them they were at the centre of your heart.

Many of us think that once we launch our business, or break even, or the financial crisis is over, we will have more time for the people we love. But realistically, that time never comes. We are not suggesting that you take a gap year now and spend every day with the people you hold dearest, although this is an option. We greatly admire those founders who were able to carve out time for this endeavour. Such is the case with Lawrence Leuschner, climate tech investor, environmentalist, CEO, and co-founder of TIER, who took parental leave when his first child was born, only to return more energised than ever to lead his company in January 2022. Think about the memories he will forever treasure, which he would never have experienced if he had waited years to make time for his family.

Making the time to nurture your special connections on a regular basis is critical. Equally important, when you do make that time, is to be fully present with your mind, heart, and body to the best of your ability. As with all great things in life, it's not about quantity; the quality of those moments matters most. Another important aspect of family relationships is to remember that this is not a competition you need to "win." This means that you may need to learn to forgive - as opposed to thinking you're better

CHAPTER THREE

"We've got this gift of love, but love is like a precious plant. You can't just accept it and leave it in the cupboard or just think it's going to get on by itself. You've got to keep watering it. You've got to really look after it and nurture it."

— John Lennon

than, if someone makes a mistake in the relationship. Maintaining unity, having a shared vision, and doing things together are what counts - not keeping score on who is right or wrong. You only have one family and, as part of it, you have a lot of responsibility.

As relationship expert, author, and therapist Katherine Woodward Thomas writes in her book, *Calling in "The One": 7 Weeks to Attract the Love of Your Life:* "To give up having to be right, having to prove someone else wrong, having to have the last word, having to be understood - that is the mark of a person who is capable and truly ready to create a loving relationship that will last and flourish over time."

Here is another fact: your business success is built on teamwork, even if you're the sole founder and CEO! In this instance, "team" refers to your life partner, not your company board. You and your partner co-create your life together, and to reach a level of excellence, you must make important decisions with a calm, clear mind so you have the energy required to navigate challenging moments in which you will need a supportive partner at home.

Conny states: "I would not have been so successful without the unconditional support and understanding of my life partner Sabine, whom I met in high school. She not only stepped up as an exemplary mother, but she was always my oasis of calm: always there, always caring, never arguing. You can only achieve that by having resilience and the willingness to compromise for the greater good of the family. That's why I always advise my younger friends to be careful about whom they marry. It's like a fifty-year loan from a bank: you make a decision that will impact every day of your life!"

However, there are situations when it's important to face reality and follow Katherine Woodward Tomas's advice: "If you are operating under the illusion that you can continue to hold on to people who you know are not good for you, and still create an extraordinary life filled with love and fulfilment, then you are fooling yourself. Toxic ties cost us, and they cost us big time. If you are feeling stuck in your life, look to see who or what it is that you are stuck to."

To provide you with some winning principles on how to thrive as a power couple - being married and business partners at the same time - we interviewed tech investors, TED-X speakers, and serial founders Katja and Michael Hengl, who, as of the writing of this book, have been married for thirty years and raised three amazing children. What they share is priceless.

Katja and Michael are living examples of the development principles they coach and teach. They expanded from the "I-space" - **How can I grow as a person?** - to the "we-space" - **How can I 10x the quality of my relationship? How can I cultivate trust and intimacy?**

"Raising our kids, leading the family, growing a competitive business, and creating life-changing experiences for our clients is a multi-tasking operation," Michael shares. When asked the question, "How did you get to know your wife?" he smiles and candidly answers, "Well, the process was to marry her. I'm discovering more and more of Katja every day, and even if it was love at first sight and it still is, it took a lot of practice not to drift apart. Because we did not follow an easy path, we were really a speed couple."

He stresses the importance of understanding that relationships are a collaboration, and each person's contribution may look different. "Nevertheless," Michael says, "you're running all on one energy source. You're a collective intelligence unit on one battery, no matter who is doing the active outgoing marketing speeches, and who is working in the background."

Katja agrees: "Taking care of the whole energy level: of both of us, our family, and our team is something which needs to be balanced constantly . . . having these conversations and not letting people off the hook when someone in the system is not well or underperforms. There is no separation! Yes, we are different individuals . . . and we are one living system, which is constantly interrelated, especially when you love each other as we do."

It was reassuring to hear them acknowledge that feelings can oscillate - and you may not always feel

love toward your partner - but in a marriage, if there's a deep connection underneath and you constantly build trust, you can work everything out.

Imagine a married couple like one social brain: brilliant only when both hemispheres join. Constant communication, connection, and integration are paramount for the success of the couple. Michael believes that "this collective intelligence starts with two people who are different, and that's often a source of conflict. Conflicts have a bad reputation. Nevertheless, they are the source of innovation and creativity. If you turn it into an attitude from 'Yes, but' and being righteous, to 'Yes, and' . . . taking one deep breath and being mindful to build on each other's ideas, you reach the magic source of co-creating rather than competing."

To understand the benefits of running a business together, Michael invites us to consider the metaphor of eyesight: "If you blindfold yourself and start seeing only with one eye, what you see with your right eye is not identical with the view from your left eye. You immediately notice that the space disappears because this is the beauty of the brain: it can process two different perspectives into one and add on the value of the space. This is the value of collective intelligence, integrating more people or more perspectives. That doesn't mean that everybody can make every decision, but we can collect more effectively what is a smart decision in comparison to risky, one-sided one, depending on the bias or mood of one person."

Katja and Michael also ask themselves, "What is success for us and how will we define it?" To answer this question, they measure the quality of their well-being in a simple, balanced scorecard:

Do I feel happy? Do you feel happy?

Is the business growing?

Is there some impact on the environment we can have, to make the world a better place?

This is a great, simple tool for all of us to use!

This power couple revealed another key ingredient to the longevity of their relationship: they renew their "marriage model" every year. Katja emphasises, "Every single year, we start with a commitment for one year. This means that if, in the middle of that year, I say, 'I'm not happy anymore with you and your behaviours,' we know that the other partner has time until the end of that year to grow into something better we are both happy with. I will not leave you; I will not have other relationships, but you have to change."

This fresh, dynamic model worked best not only for their marriage but also as a personal motivation to constantly evolve into better versions of themselves as individuals. "We did change it once, to a lifetime commitment," confessed Katja, "and it didn't work. So, our model is to commit for one year. You cannot leave the contract, and you need to do your best to make it work during that year. Stay true and faithful, even in crisis." Besides this continuous reinvention, Katja and Michael acknowledge that another pre-requisite is absolute transparency and honesty.

We asked Alina Lazarescu-Abboud, angel investor, entrepreneur, mother of three, and married to a successful entrepreneur, what she would recommend in order to have a thriving family life. She says, "There is no single formula for all couples. You need to know that your contribution, your role, is yours to define, as long as you keep in mind that you are part of a team, and you are building something together." There are no right or wrong answers.

Her husband, Walid Abboud, a successful serial entrepreneur and investor, agrees that in a couple, the good of the whole often outweighs the individual's needs. "I was blessed to find the right life partner, but that was not the end of the story - it was just the beginning!" According to Walid, the key skill you need to develop to have a successful marriage is spiritual intelligence. You need to keep things in perspective, through the lens of a common purpose, evolving together energetically, and constantly making the effort to grow together. "You cannot not evolve!" said Walid. "Even if you're not aware of it, or you resist changing, every day, something around you evolves. And if you don't keep pace with it, you shouldn't be surprised when you're left behind, both in business and personal life."

Alina stresses the importance of viewing the commitment to a long-term journey as the compass that keeps two people together. "We somehow expect that, if two people love each other, everything should be super-easy. You're together, building a family, with the best intentions at the start, so what could go wrong? We all know how important communication is, and, at the same time, without doing

The key skill you need to develop to have a successful marriage is spiritual intelligence.

your inner work, you will hear what your partner is saying through the lens of your own wounds and trauma - and get triggered by the least important words or actions. When I understood that I could transform my relationship just by healing myself, I felt like Einstein discovering the formula for energy!"

Summarising the key elements contributing day-to-day to their happiness, Alina and Walid stress the importance of openness towards each other. "We maintain constant communication with each other. Even when there is not enough time, we know that there is that openness, like an energy channel connecting us. That's important because, when that channel is closed, even if you talk forever, your message and emotions do not reach the other partner. It is like keeping your heart open." This constant work they do, individually and together, helps them evolve spiritually. "We create intimate experiences together, from restarting to going out on a date once our youngest daughter grew old enough, to going to meditation retreats together. And last but not least is the care we have for each other, the one you feel in your heart even if you don't talk so much about it. It's in the tone of our voice, even when we're super busy."
You may think that the best way to improve relationships is to focus on the other person exclusively, but that is not 100 per cent true; it is equally critical to do the inner work on your own to maintain

thriving relationships. For example, Alina shared that everything changed for her when she understood during a relationships course that sometimes "you don't need two to tango. Controversial statement, right? I felt the same, and I cannot emphasise enough how grateful I am that I was brave to stay and do all the inner work required, to finally understand the essence of this principle. Many women are always waiting for the man in their life to read their minds, do everything to make them happy, you know, take us to the moon and back and sweep us off our feet. And if we're honest, that is pure teenager thinking. By doing that relationship course, I faced and healed my wounds and trauma, and a new perspective on life opened for me. I gave up expecting Walid to behave as I wanted and dedicate his life to making me happy. I discovered that by offering myself attention and appreciation and care, I can be an adult in our relationship, enjoying it without being needy and wanting everything from my husband." We are entirely in alignment with Alina's point of view.

This principle is true for men as well. Despite his busy schedule, Walid shared his commitment to personal growth as the key ingredient to the accomplished couple he and Alina are: "I believe it is my responsibility to invest my time and constantly educate myself, in order to be the best husband and father – that I can be. Being present when I am with my children and wife is non-negotiable."

The benefits of doing this work are incredibly rewarding, as Alina points out: "The more present you are and the more you work on your own issues, the more you become aware and awakened. And the more your consciousness gets activated, the more you can be present and develop superpowers in connecting with your loved ones. This is what I am practising now: being intentional to receive what is present in the space between us and paying attention to the very subtle energies, and see what comes up from there - that is a source of creation."

Reflection Questions:

- How much time, attention and energy do you give those at the centre of your life?

- Do they know how important they are to you?

- Are you present at the key moments in their lives?

- What can you do to make this relationship even better?

"I've learned that people will forget what you said, people will forget what you did, but people will never forget how you made them feel."

— Maya Angelou

The Second Layer: Your Trusted Friends

"Lots of people want to ride with you in the limo, but what you want is someone who will take the bus with you when the limo breaks down."

— Oprah Winfrey

Surrounding yourself with encouraging friends is very important. If your family is not supportive of your business ambitions, your close friends become even more important. Conny was blessed with a supportive father who also became his best friend and was always an inspiration to him. He continues to be his mentor, even now in his late eighties. Every year, they have their special time together, either in a health resort like Lanserhof, or on a cruise with MS Europa 2.

It is crucial to find out who will truly support you; not all the people who are ready to celebrate with you will be there when you struggle. Some people in your circle might be more discouraging than supportive, or even make fun of you. Our view on this is very similar to what Mark Twain stated almost 200 years ago: "Keep away from people who try to belittle your ambitions. Small people always do that, but the really great [ones] make you feel that you, too, can become great."

As an entrepreneur, it is essential to have special people you trust and have deep connections with. People who are always there for you, believing in you even when you lose hope - people who care about you enough to tell you the unpleasant truths, help you get back on track when you're wrong, and stand by you while you get your act together. They will call you with a heartfelt, "Are you OK? Do you want to talk about it?" followed by, "I am here for you! How can I help now?"

"People are lonely because they build walls instead of bridges."

— Joseph F. Newton

These people are your sounding board. You know they love and appreciate you unconditionally. Just talking to them makes you feel lighter, and they give you a more balanced perspective on something that looked overwhelming just minutes before. It doesn't matter who they are - friends or family members - but if you don't have them, you will want to start looking to find that kind of friend, coach, or mentor.

Reflection Questions:

- Who are the people you trust the most?

- And how are you contributing to that relationship?

CHAPTER THREE

The Third Layer: Close Business Partners

Seventy years ago, after the end of WWII, people could easily start companies alone. Today, due to the complexity of the current business environment and the breadth of skills required to found and manage a business, starting a company has become a team effort. We see more and more unicorn businesses with two to three founders, who blend their selling, finance, and innovation skills. From Walid Aboud's perspective, "To get your marriage wrong . . . it's hell. Although something worse, in my view, is to get your business partner wrong - a spouse you can still divorce, but sometimes you cannot get out of a toxic business partnership." As a business angel and investor, Conny pays close attention to discover the exceptional entrepreneur who would serve as the forefront, and also ensures that the start-up or company has the right team members before giving them his trust.

Even if you don't have a co-founder, you can think of the person or people in your team who are essential for the success of your business. Be honest with yourself and examine the quality of your relationship with them.

Reflection Questions:

Think about your team and ask yourself:

- Do we trust and respect each other?

- Do we have clear agreements on how we work together?

- Do we share the same values?

Your peace of mind, the quality of your time spent at work, and the success of your business depends on the quality of these relationships. Fortunately, it's never too late to have that honest conversation, reset expectations, and commit to the required change.

"When you stop expecting people to be perfect,
you can like them for who they are."

— Donald Miller

Your Network

Most likely, you have heard the quote attributed to author and motivational speaker Jim Rohn: "You're the average of the five people you spend the most time with." How true this is! Author David Burkus takes this one step further. In his book, *Friend of a Friend . . .: Understanding the Hidden Networks That Can Transform Your Life and Your Career,* Burkus states, "You're not the average of the FIVE people you surround yourself with. It's way bigger than that. You're the average of all the people who surround you. So, take a look around and make sure you're in the right surroundings."[1]

We hope this illustrates the importance of networking and the huge impact relationships have in your business life. It also explains why some of the most intelligent people you knew in high school may not have become the most successful people later in life - if they couldn't connect with others.

> **Who you know becomes as important - if not more - than what you know.**

Conny became aware of the impact of networking very early in life. During his years in school, he witnessed how important it was to be connected to the right people. Then, in the business world, he learned that networking is just as essential to being successful as it was in school. Conny says, "Knowing exactly who to contact at any moment in time is key in life. Having the smartest business idea is not enough: it is knowing the right people who can help you sell your product and build relationships in your target markets that will make your business successful or not. In general, people put much more effort into learning new things than in building a network."

What we're not taught in school is that Who you know becomes as important - if not more - than what you know. Investors want to deal with people they like, people they know and trust. When you hire someone for a key role, or you need to externalise a process, it always helps to have your decision validated by someone you trust and respect in that area.

Despite having access to new technology, the human factor remains essential. Many believe they can find the best people through platforms like LinkedIn or Instagram. In some cases, this might work, but oftentimes, some of the best connections are difficult to reach - and they have skilled "gatekeepers" who protect them. Therefore, the bigger the network you have, the higher your chances of finding the perfect person to help you (or introduce you to the right person). In fact, Conny goes so far as to state, "I have not seen that many people become successful without having a long list of personal contacts." Michael Hengl provides this piece of brilliant advice: "Don't be a star, be a galaxy." Connection is

---

1 - Burkus, David, "You're NOT the Average of the Five People You Surround Yourself With," *Medium*, May 23, 2018, https://medium.com/the-mission/youre-not-the-average-of-the-five-people-you-surround-yourself-with-f21b817f6e69.

essential for growth, and research confirms it. An eight-year-long study conducted in Israel during the dotcom boom revealed that the few software start-ups that survived the crash were the ones that built a strong communication network with others like them. In retrospect, the "'club of winners' could have been predicted based on how they built their network."[2]

"The true value of networking doesn't come from how many people we can meet but rather how many people we can introduce to others."

— Simon Sinek

At this point, you may be asking yourself, "I understand the importance of networking, but how can I do it properly - especially if this is not a strength of mine?" First, you must understand that networking is more of an attitude than a skill. It is a mindset that involves seeing every person you meet as an opportunity to grow and learn, and you absolutely must start meeting people. Even if you don't currently feel comfortable establishing new relationships, you can learn the art of networking! We have listed some tips below to get you started. Once you incorporate these ideas into your daily routine, you'll soon be networking with the best of us!

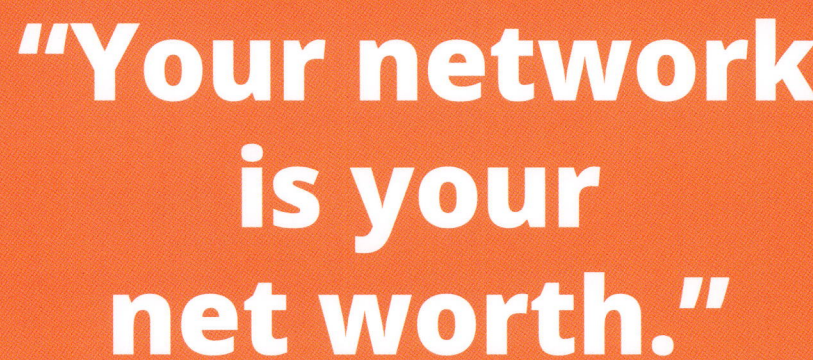

"Your network is your net worth."

— Porter Gale

2 - Raz, Ornit and Peter A. Gloor, "Size Really Matters: New Insights for Start-Ups' Survival," *Management Science* 53, no. 2 (2007): pgs. 169-77. http://www.jstor.org/stable/20110688

Networking Tips

1

Just do it.
Networking is more of an attitude than a skill. Start meeting people. Be intentional in your presence. Make it a habit on any occasion to simply introduce yourself to people you don't know. Be curious about the other person and listen. Cultivate diverse connections, seeking people from various industries, backgrounds, and experiences, to gain fresh perspectives and opportunities.

2

Be a giver not a taker.
Be less focused on what you get out of that conversation and more on how all parties could benefit. As Adam Grant said in *Give and Take: Why Helping Others Drives Our Success*, "From a relationship perspective, givers build deeper and broader connections." Offer help and support without expecting an immediate return. When you give, you are doing this for yourself, not for others! If you consider yourself to be an over-giver and are frustrated that you give away too much, remember that networking means reciprocity, too. Don't shy away from advocating for your own interests - people love helping others.

3

Show up daily.
Networking is a life-long journey, not a short, intense communication campaign you use in case of a business emergency. The sooner you start loving it, the sooner you will enjoy the dividends it pays over time. Therefore, consider networking like a savings box you must pay in every day. The more you make it a daily habit to reach out and connect with others, the more comfortable you will become with networking. The more people in your network, the more empowered and independent you will feel, too.

4

See networking as an investment.
Networking is time and energy-consuming, and like everything in life, it is not always fun. However, if you consider each interaction with interest and give it a chance, you will discover parts of networking you thoroughly enjoy. Remember that there is no bad meeting; you can always find something positive - even if it's simply a lesson you've learned about how to interact with other people in a better way.

5

Be strategic and creative.
Relevant industry events, trade shows, conferences, and parties are essential networking venues. But don't forget that networking can be done anywhere. Conny found that the best places for networking are where people are comfortable and relaxed, and he particularly likes meeting new people during a flight. If you are in a place where people are in a good mood and open for connection, all you have to do is be nice and act genuinely interested. Think about it: you never know who you will be talking to and whether that person will be valuable to you at some point in life. Always have your business card or electronic equivalent ready, since you never know when you're going to make your next connection!

Conny says, "Taking advantage of my strength as a natural born networker, I have built a reputation so big that my connections are now part of my assets, part of my wealth. Realising the value and importance of my network, I knew that I needed to start bringing people together. This is how Unternehmertag (The Entrepreneur's Day) was born in 2007. It is a unique event in Europe, where 600 handpicked entrepreneurs, investors, representatives of influential families, business angels, CEOs and personalities from business, politics, and entertainment come together for three days at an exclusive resort on the shores of Tegernsee in Germany. A few years later, I created Angelgate, an exclusive circle of business angels, who meet regularly to share and select investment opportunities, taking advantage of their know-how to support and learn from each other.

"Finally, every December, I invite sixty to seventy friends to have fun together in the mountains, for a ski break. For many, this is the highlight event of the year, as we wouldn't have opportunities to meet otherwise."

Reflection Questions:

- Is networking your strength?

- What can you do to improve in your networking?

- If networking is new to you, what are the first steps you need to take to start building your network?

CHAPTER THREE

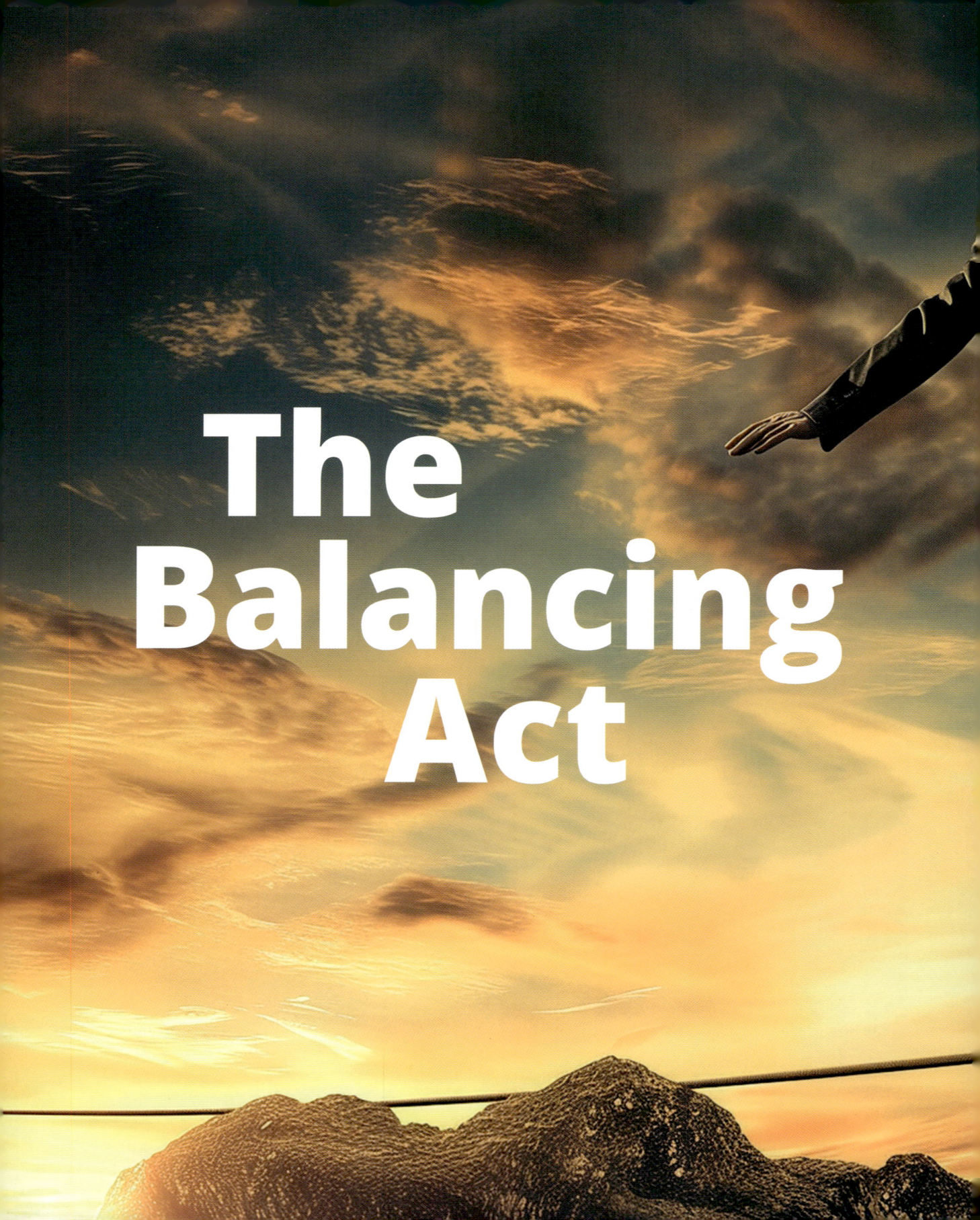

The Balancing Act

Although, as entrepreneurs, we are essentially "married to our businesses," in the last moments of our lives, we will regret not the business meetings we missed, but the magical moments we did not live with the people we love. We often wish we could go back in time and arrive at the hospital for the birth of our child, attend that graduation ceremony, or spend an extra day with our parents before they left this world. Therefore, always consider how to be present with the people closest to you - the centre of your onion - while focusing on your work and the time-consuming networking that supports your success as an entrepreneur. Take some time now and ask yourself: What are the non-negotiable commitments I'm ready to make to ensure I am giving those closest to me the quality time and attention they deserve?

As you clarify your non-negotiables, keep in mind the vision you have for the relationships that are most important to you. When Alina and Walid Abboud started their relationship fourteen years ago, they decided to set an intention: "Our relationship is like a great adventure, a spiritual companionship filled with passion and fun. And great adventure for us was not about travelling the world and living in different places, although we have done that too, but it was about inner discovery. This spirit of exploration and growing together mindset allowed us to go through the ups and downs of any marriage. This vision needed refinement over time but, at the core, it is still true for us."

Alina continues, "Some people value diversity in the way they experience life, so being with different people is the right answer for them. For me, stability and having that deep human connection is important. This is what motivates me to be committed to my life partner (and the vision we have together as a couple). You might think it's harder to keep it fresh, because you could get stuck in routines - and that it's quite laborious to do the inner work throughout your life. But for me, it would be more challenging to date somebody else every six months. It's too much! I prefer to invest my energy in my partnership for life with Walid, my kids, and my business."

"Like a great athlete, we must have a very clear vision of what we want to accomplish before we make a move. Vision, in preparation for an action, is as important as the action itself."

— Marianne Williamson

Once your vision is clear, start listing the immediate actions you can take to improve in this area over the next couple of months. This could be as easy as spending quality time with your children or working with a relationship coach to get over that break-up, divorce, or business exit that is keeping you awake at night. The time to address whatever is eroding your peace of mind is now.

Another balancing act you need to consider is the quantity and quality of your relationships. For many years, networking for Conny was about connecting with as many people as possible, all over the world. He used to say: "Relationships are only harming those who don't have them." Once Dorina introduced him to the concept of The Golden Circle - the people you admire, trust, respect and want to spend your time with - he decided to focus on creating deeper connections with the people who inspire him the most. "It took twenty to thirty years to find what I am looking for. The better I know myself, the clearer my selection criteria for close connections become. As my time and energy are finite, I need to have the courage to let go of old friends as well, to make space for new connections, aligned with who I am now."

As you evolve as an entrepreneur and as a person, some of your friends will not be able to keep up with your transformation. You might experience what Michelle Obama shared in her Netflix interview with Oprah, about some of her friends who "Lost oxygen, couldn't make the climb." We invite you to open your heart and trust that many of your best friends are yet to come.

"Depth of friendship does not depend on length of acquaintance."

— Rabindranath Tagore

LET'S REVIEW

This chapter emphasised the importance of relationships and networking. As for your relationships, you can envision an onion, with those closest to you at the centre. This visualisation can help you remain aligned with your vision to spend quality time being present with those who are most important in your life.

Networking is essential to your success as an entrepreneur as well, so it is critical that you get out into the world each day and build your network. We provided some simple tips to get you started, especially if networking is outside of your comfort zone.

Finally, we have provided you with some guiding questions that will help you balance your personal and professional lives in a way that helps you not just survive but thrive.

WHAT'S NEXT

Relationships and networking are key ingredients to a fulfilling life, resulting in both personal and professional success. With this in mind, we will explore how to take what you are learning and apply it to every facet of your life, from personal and work-related relationships, to material possessions and experiences. By taking action to elevate your life in all areas, you will enjoy an extraordinary quality of life - the topic of our next chapter.

CHAPTER FOUR

Quality of Life:
Deliberate Choices for a Fulfilling Life Experience

"Let your soul be a magnet for magical moments, and watch as the universe responds with delightful surprises"

— Author unknown

MAGIC MOMENTS THAT LAST A LIFETIME

When you look back at the life you have lived, you will not remember your everyday existence. In fact, it has been said that when you are on your deathbed, you only remember approximately ten of the best moments in your life. I call these "magic moments," and I must admit I became addicted to creating and experiencing them.

Reflecting on my best moments, I realised they were not the ones I expected. That's because magic moments are not always the major milestones - like the birth of a child or a wedding. Instead, magic moments can be as simple as dancing in the sun, or sitting in your favourite restaurant on the beach, on a rainy day, with your feet in the sand, with the person you love. Magic moments can captivate you so completely that you might be having dinner in a Michelin restaurant and be so present and connected with the person in front of you, that you completely forget to eat.

While these magic moments are different for everybody, reflecting on them is important. Sadly, when I ask people about their magic moments, very often, they struggle to remember or to describe them. And those who stick with the cliched moments, like graduations, weddings, and births, often share that these moments are, in fact, quite stressful! The way I would describe a magic moment is that you are in complete flow and connectedness for hours or even days: when you forget about time, worries, and your mind becomes free.

How can we create magic moments? By opening our hearts, being fully present, and feeling grateful for the experience we are in. We live in our heads so much of the time that we often forget to connect with our hearts and all our senses. Life in itself is magic if we only let it flow through us.

Another belief I have is that magic moments are nothing if they cannot be shared with the right people. After I sold my first unicorn company twenty years ago, I wanted to enjoy life to the fullest. But I felt exhausted and empty. Even when I was ringing the bell at the stock exchange, there was so much excitement mixed with worry, wondering if everything would work out. Once I finally realised that it had all gone to plan and I would be financially independent for the rest of my life, I felt a mixture of pure bliss and relief. I had reached the peak of my career at an extremely young age and wanted to celebrate the fact that I had "made it."

I wanted to make up for all the suffering and hard work I had endured. I began to buy nice cars and

expensive watches, looked for houses in places all over the world and wanted to travel to the most exotic locations. I remember going to the Burj-Al-Arab in Dubai, the best hotel in the world at the time, taking a helicopter from the airport to the hotel roof to get to my 300-square-metre suite. I opened the curtains and saw the astonishing view, opened a bottle of Petrus, ordered a pizza, and watched my favourite Harry Potter movie. In those moments, even though everything was exactly the way I wanted to be, I felt lonely. No one was there to share that experience with. It became clear that those special times are nothing if they cannot be shared.

— *Conny*

CHAPTER FOUR

WHAT IS QUALITY OF LIFE?

French surgeon and Nobel Prize winner Alexis Carrel once said, "The quality of life is more important than life itself." Not only is this true, but we could probably dedicate an entire book to quality of life - and how to improve it.

Irrespective of where we come from, where we live, and the chapter of life we are in, we are constantly trying to improve our quality of life. In fact, this quest for a better quality of life has driven human behaviour for thousands of years. It is one of the reasons economies function - and why we send our children to certain schools. We are all seeking a better life, whether we do this consciously or subconsciously. And when it comes to our own children, we want to offer them the best quality of life we can.

But how do we define "quality of life"? We believe quality of life is about what makes life worth living: your overall life experience, how you enjoy each day, how safe you feel, and how much happiness and fulfilment you find. Everything we discuss in this book comes together to elevate your quality of life, from your health, well-being, and connection with yourself and others, to the environment you live in, how much time you spend doing the things you love, your ability to explore and seek adventure, and the magical moments you experience. Ultimately, your quality of life reflects who you are, the environment you create and live in, and who you become.

The University of Toronto's Quality of Life Model illustrates how the three essential dimensions - *Being, Belonging, and Becoming* - interconnect and interact to shape an individual's overall quality of life.

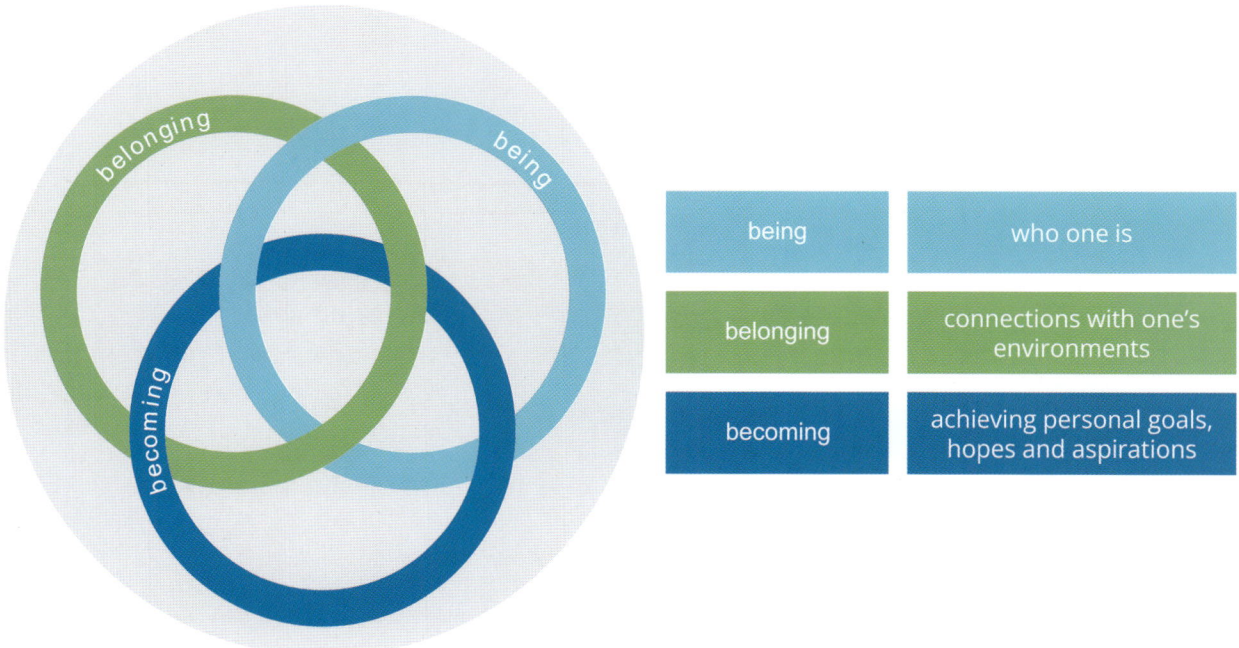

being	who one is
belonging	connections with one's environments
becoming	achieving personal goals, hopes and aspirations

Quality of life (QoL) across the areas of Being, Belonging, and Becoming is measured by "the relative importance or meaning attached to each particular dimension and the extent of the person's enjoyment with respect to each dimension. In this way . . . [QoL] is adapted to the lives of all humans, at any time, and from their individual perspectives."[1]

One way to evaluate your quality of life is by asking yourself at the end of each day:

Was today a good day? Did I achieve what I wanted? What have I learned? How did I feel? Did I enjoy my day? If this were the last day, week, or month of my life, what would I do?

Asking yourself these questions can help uncover the things you always wanted to do . . . but only after "urgent" matters were completed. By asking yourself these questions, you might realise that the time to do those "someday" items is now. The urgent "to-do list," however, never ends: when one problem is solved, another one will take its place.

We often do not realise how easy it is to postpone what is important because we feel the pressure to deal with urgent matters. We are too busy, and then we become too tired - and the day we get to enjoy our wish list may never arrive.

Reflection Questions:

- What do you envision when contemplating your desired quality of life?

- Where do you want to live and work?

- What will make you feel that you have made the most of each day?

- What do you want to experience daily?

- What changes do you need to make, to improve your quality of life?

Regrets of the Dying

"In the end, we only regret the chances we didn't take, relationship we were afraid to have, and the decisions we waited too long to make."

— Lewis Carroll

A few years ago, at the Entrepreneurs' Day at Lake Tegernsee in Germany, Conny gifted each of the 600 attendees the book that was the catalyst for him to start redefining the way he lives his life: *The Top Five Regrets of the Dying*, by Bronnie Ware. Reading this book can help you ensure that you will not harbour these regrets during the final days of your life:[2]

---

1 - University of Toronto, "Quality of Life Model," Quality of Life Research Unit, accessed January 15, 2024, http://sites.utoronto.ca/qol/qol_model.htm.
2 - Ware, Bonnie, *The Top Five Regrets of the Dying: A Life Transformed by the Dearly Departing*, Hay House, 2011.

TOP FIVE REGRETS OF THE DYING

1 I wish I'd had the courage to live a life true to myself, not the life others expected of me.

2 I wish I hadn't worked so hard.

3 I wish I'd had the courage to express my feelings.

4 I wish I had stayed in touch with my friends.

5 I wish I had let myself be happier.

From *Mindful*'s interview with Bronnie Ware, author of *The Top Five Regrets of the Dying*.

For more info visit mindful.org/noregrets.

Becoming aware of these regrets is only the first step; we need to make a conscious effort to break out of old, unhelpful patterns We are so conditioned by our parents, teachers, and society to live in a certain way and follow certain rules. And many times, we don't even realise how our subconscious beliefs are driving our lives. Conny remarks: "While this book had a profound impact on me, I also realised how difficult it is to live in a way in which you are sure you will not have those regrets. I am still on a journey to find my own truth - who am I, beyond my conditionings." Sadly, if we continue to live our lives on autopilot, we may find ourselves experiencing regret when it's too late to make a change. However, if you begin to contemplate what is truly important to you, it is possible to wake up and start challenging the concept that there is only one "correct" way to live.

What Is Most Important to You?

When asked what is important to us, most of us will answer with reference to health, love, safety, or other intangibles. Yet, many of us spend the majority of our money on things. If we reflect on the material things we desire, we are often influenced by the adverts we see, societal trends, and the desire to fit in. So much noise contaminates our thoughts, telling us what we need, that we blindly buy what is sold to us. We all know that we don't necessarily need all those things. But finding the right balance between excessive consumerism, basic material needs, and emotional fulfilment is not easy.

Before buying your next car, watch, or the latest shoes, ask yourself this: "Am I missing anything more important? Can I spend this money in a way that will give me more long-term satisfaction?" Most of the time, a brief conversation with someone you trust can steer you towards the choice that brings you closer to what is actually important to you.

Improving Your Quality of Life . . . Right Now

Conny is very clear about what quality of life means to him: "It's the freedom to choose: what I want to work on, when I want to work, where I want to work, and how I want my surroundings to be. My space reflects my needs and my values, and wherever I spend more of my time, I want to feel at home. That is why I have a few places I can call home - where I have a spa and gym, a wine cellar, a cosy living area, beautiful views, and a nice hiking trail nearby.

"I choose to travel often, so I can interact with different cultures, enjoy nature, and have extraordinary experiences. When I travel, I carefully choose the hotels where I stay. And if a hotel does not feel comfortable or satisfying, I don't hesitate to change it. I travel light and never check in my luggage, to be able to travel quickly and easily. Even when I take a train, which is not my favourite, I make it a memorable experience.

"One essential ingredient that enriches my quality of life is music. Music helps me relax, recover, and experience a wide range of emotions. I sometimes spend hours creating playlists for different occasions, and I often carry a speaker with me when I go for a hike or when I travel.

"Lack of direction, not lack of time, is the problem. We all have twenty-four-hour days."

— Zig Ziglar

"Another key ingredient of my quality of life is laughing and having fun. I always say that life is too short to be taken so seriously. I try to find humour in everyday situations, and I have a few good jokes about nearly any topic. I even have a small notebook where I write down the best jokes I've heard, because I believe laughing is an essential part of a healthy and happy life. It not only promotes physical and emotional well-being but also enhances our relationships and contributes to a more positive and optimistic outlook on life. But most of all, I want to create magic moments."

Henry Cookson, the explorer and founder of Cookson Adventures you met in chapter two, shares how he improves his quality of life and creates extraordinary moments by interacting with people while they are out in nature, in amazing places, and immersed in different cultures. This is the essence of a high-quality life for him. Instead of engaging in a desperate chase to create experiences, Cookson believes in creating memories during the limited time we have on Earth. Authenticity is the thread that runs through the story of his life. Disregarding what society pressures us to look or behave like, Henry remains true to his commitment to be who he really is, without airbrushing his public image to build a false, more marketable persona.

"There is only one person responsible for the quality of life you live . . . and that person is you."

— Jack Canfield

When we don't have the courage to improve our quality of life, sometimes unexpected, dramatic events will teach us a lesson. COVID-19 forced us to rethink many aspects of our lives - and some of them were for the better! Many of us discovered that we can work from anywhere in the world and that we need much less to be happy than we previously believed. Although remote working was technically possible before the pandemic, the accepted belief was that we needed to be in an office, for ten to twelve hours a day, to feel productive. Forced by lockdowns to redesign our lives, we realised how old-fashioned, outdated, and counter-productive these rules really were.

The key takeaway here is that we always have a choice in how to create our life. Established patterns might seem set in stone, but shift your perspective, and they will lose power, making way for new directions.
To make that a reality, consider Denis Waitley's advice: "Since the mind is a specific bio-computer, it needs specific instructions and directions." You get to decide which instructions you want to give your mind. To start designing the life you really want, you need to brainstorm your vision, get clear about your strategies, and take action to create the quality of life you want.

"Don't limit yourself. Many people limit themselves
to what they think they can do. You can go as far as your mind lets you.
What you believe, remember, you can achieve."

— Mary Kay Ash

To elevate your quality of life, you must adopt a comprehensive approach, and including your sense of being, becoming, and belonging. It can be as simple as living in the moment. We often live in the past or in the future when we think or talk about our quality of life: what we want to do when we have more time and money. It's okay to be focused and full of energy chasing the next goal as long as we appreciate what we have right now! The key is to remind yourself to breathe deeply and consciously feel the richness of every second.

Improving your quality of life can be a meaningful, enjoyable challenge, which will evolve in time. Start by envisioning the life you want to have. Then be intentional, every day, taking small actions, and feel like you already live your vision.

Reflection Questions:

- What is the first step you can take right now to improve your quality of life?

- What are the low-hanging fruits which will have an immediate and positive effect?

- What are you committing to do, to make your vision a reality?

Be creative and think ouside the box!

THE ULTIMATE DIMENSION OF QUALITY OF LIFE

It is impossible to discuss quality of life without acknowledging the importance of clean air, fresh water, rich soil, and the immense variety of species that directly or indirectly sustain our existence. We all live on one planet, and we are intrinsically connected to her. Planet Earth is the only home we have, and it provides - free of charge - everything we need to live, thrive, and evolve as a species. There is no shareholding for the capital our planet offers for free. The question is: what do we give back in this exchange to make it sustainable for us and the generations to come?

For Henry Cookson, quality of life is "being able to see the glory and the unimaginable beauty of planet Earth and how it interacts with us. And sharing this life force with loved ones and strangers, old and new friends, or business partners."

We do take Earth for granted.

Henry highlights, "We do take Earth for granted. From art and fashion, people talking about their inspiration for designs and colours, to technologies, to medicines - everything is inspired by the nature around us. We don't give nature the credit it's due. We often believe it's our own brilliance and our own entrepreneurial skills, but it comes from the very primordial oneness

that we all came from, and all the beauty and the magic around us." He aims to wake us up to the splendour around us and, at the same time, to the state of our planet, the destruction and the cost of everything we build, every journey we make, and everything we grow and consume.

If every company has a set of values and a mission statement, Henry believes that "part of that mission statement should be to protect our home, protecting Planet Earth with everything we do." Like him, we understand that a start-up, a small business that is growing, may not have the bandwidth to do all the good things they want. And herein lies the solution: "In this race for profit, when we're deciding what's going to get sacrificed first, can we aim for the Earth to take a bit less impact?"

The 2022 WWF (World Wildlife Fund) Living Planet Report shows a 69 per cent average decline in wildlife populations since 1970, with wildlife populations in Latin America and the Caribbean dropping at a staggering rate of 94 per cent, while freshwater species populations have suffered an 83 per cent drop.[3]

Super-heating in the Pacific and natural disasters like hurricanes and floods are our reality today. Furthermore, Henry warns us about the many different varieties of species that have disappeared: "The small little things that don't make the headlines, like a whale or a dolphin or a rhino, are an important part of our fabric too. When you drove a car in the countryside twenty years ago, your headlights and your windscreen would be covered by insects. That's now a rarity because we've poisoned our countryside. It still looks beautiful, but when you look under the surface, you notice that the little things, the fabric of what our ecosystem is based on, is gone."

---

3 - "69% Average Decline in Wildlife Populations Since 1970, Says New WWF Report," World Wildlife Fund, press release, 13 October, 2022, https://www.worldwildlife.org/press-releases/69-average-decline-in-wildlife-populations-since-1970-says-new-wwf-report.

Having placed conservation at the heart of his extraordinary journeys, Henry finds this reality very difficult: "Human behaviour is not going to change enough. People are too comfortable to change things. Even though it's around the corner, psychologically, it's harder to see something further in the future. We'll deal with it another time. So it's terrifying. Here we have this slow-moving car crash of climate change on our planet, yet we're only doing small, insignificant things which aren't stopping this inevitable steamroller. You always need a systemic shock to challenge the status quo and make people realise that things are really dark."

Let's prevent the scenario where future generations pay the exorbitant bill of our overconsumption, waste, and negligence.

At the same time, reflecting on the 2020 pandemic, he knows that we have the ability to change: "We changed our behaviour as a species almost overnight with COVID. And because we've done that, it didn't reach the predicted impact, like the global Spanish flu had. As awful as COVID was to a lot of people, losing loved ones, it was a wake-up call for many to start prioritising what is truly important in their lives." Reflecting on the massive mobilisation of resources and alignment between key players, we can see that when there's a will, there is a way.

You don't have to be in the second half of life, and you don't need to wait to accumulate a massive amount of wealth to start taking action. When we interviewed Lila Behr, a student at the Hult International Business School in San Francisco, founder of the NGO Gaia Protection, and co-founder of the social enterprise Gaia Gives, she attributed her passion for environmentalism to travelling from an early age with her mother, experiencing the tapestry of diverse countries and cultures. Whether it was teaching children in Tanzania or Costa Rica, leading workshops on the Sustainable Development Goals in Indian schools, spearheading a circular economy project in Indonesia, gaining wisdom from indigenous elders, establishing a youth-led NGO, or co-founding a social start-up, Lila is contributing extensively to preserving our planet.

She takes her inspiration from the concept of planetary boundaries developed by the Stockholm Resilience Centre in 2009, highlighting the areas where humanity needs to ensure continued development and success for future generations. "We find ourselves at a critical juncture and must make the right decisions today to shape a future that is worth living," Lila believes. "As a global family, we need to expand our understanding of development beyond material standards alone. We must prioritise human well-being and environmental sustainability. To achieve this, it is crucial to establish resilient communities that focus on the sustainable management of biodiversity, soil, and water resources. These communities will serve as models for progress and sustainability as we move forward."

With humbleness and a deep understanding of human nature, as well as the impact that advertising, branding, and social media have on us, Henry believes that "If you're fortunate and intelligent enough, and driven, after being a very successful entrepreneur, the world is your oyster. But how many cars, how many watches, how many haute couture dresses, how many properties, how many wine collections, or trophy partners do you need? There should be a finite limit to that, and the sooner you realise that this is just a run after the dopamine hit, to cover a hole in your soul, the better. We have all bought things in the past, thinking, 'Wow, this will make me happy,' just to realize after a few months or even days that we are back to square one, craving the next best thing."

Henry invites us to at least stop and acknowledge that the success we have in life, which enables us to have what we want and travel to the destinations we dreamed of, is because of the gifts Mother Earth keeps on giving. "For the ones who have the fortune of success, just pause and ponder: *What do I owe this to?* It's not just your own genius! It's not just your contacts, your ability to get deals done, or being able to see opportunities! It's because this Earth has given us that inspiration and is constantly giving you air to breathe and food to eat . . . and maybe something needs to be given back. From that place of privilege, consider how you can respect and protect the planet. The entrepreneurs who've made a success of their lives can now put their energies into the reality of our world and what that means for their children and their grandchildren."

If you're already a trailblazer when it comes to stopping Planet Earth's destruction, or if we stirred your curiosity, triggering a sense of urgency with our guests' opinions and actions, now is your time to pause and reflect.

Reflection Questions:

- How can you become an active player in this field?

- What can you start or stop doing to have a positive impact on our planet?

"Only if we understand, will we care. Only if we care, will we help. Only if we help shall all be saved."

— Jane Goodall

LET'S REVIEW

In this chapter, you learned about the importance of creating magic moments to improve the overall quality of your life. You also learned about the importance of making your dreams a reality right now - in order to live a life without regrets. What's more, once you start living the life of your dreams, you will be in a position to consider ways in which you can make a massive and positive impact on planet Earth, regardless of where you currently are in life. Best of all, when you elevate the quality of your life, you will find yourself living a life of freedom - without a single regret!

WHAT'S NEXT

At this point, you may be reading about some of our strategies and thinking, "That's great - but how do I afford the things and experiences that I would like to bring into my ideal life?" To tackle this question, turn the page to learn more about financial independence, and how this can be the doorway to freedom and living the life you truly desire.

CHAPTER FIVE

Attain Financial Independence:
The Freedom to Live Your Life

"When you understand that your self-worth is not determined by your net-worth, then you'll have financial freedom."

— Suze Orman

RISK, REWARD, REPEAT
How Fortune Favours the Bold

In the early years of being an entrepreneur, the key ingredient to my financial freedom was the belief that I had nothing to lose, so I entered business deal negotiations with a maximum degree of confidence. I knew that regardless of the outcome, I would always have my skills and talent. With this mindset, I stopped limiting myself. I would go so far as to "spend money I didn't have," being so confident in my skills to generate the necessary financial resources. My experiences confirm the principle that first, you need to believe you are financially free before you can attract financial abundance into your life.

I remember when I started my first unicorn company, ACG, receiving the first massive order of security chips from a client. I didn't know where I was going to source them from - nor did I have any idea how I would be able to pay for them. Nevertheless, I accepted the order, trusting I would find a solution. In the following days, I worked day and night, calling and meeting hundreds of my contacts until I found the supplier and the money I needed. The decision I took, with confidence in my skills coupled with the chance I was given, helped me take the company to the next level. Once I made my first exit, however, I suddenly became more risk-averse, as I didn't want to lose what I gained through so much hard work.

For many years after that, my biggest mistake was being too much of a "chicken" - I was afraid of taking big risks. Instead of putting my early money into start-ups, I put it into real estate and securities. If I had followed my instincts, and invested in start-ups, I would probably have had much more financial success. The technology markets expanded massively from 2002 to 2008, and I had opportunities to invest in Uber, LinkedIn, and Facebook at very early stages.

It took me a long time to understand that I had lost that important, winning mindset. Out of the thirty to forty unicorn companies I have seen over the past decade, I have invested in one or two of them. In the future, my intention is to triple or quadruple the likelihood of getting it right by investing in three or four unicorns.

The importance of financial freedom is not only that you feel secure, but that you can also make better business decisions and follow your gut when it comes to investments that can pay off big time.

— Conny

IS IT TIME TO QUESTION YOUR BELIEFS ABOUT MONEY?

"Money is only a tool. It will take you wherever you wish, but it will not replace you as the driver."

— Ayn Rand

One of humanity's most impactful inventions in the last five thousand years has been the concept of money. It has played a pivotal role in facilitating the exchange of goods, ensuring fair compensation for labour, fostering economic development, building relationships of all types for individuals, communities, and organisations, and opening borders between nations. However, it is quite interesting to note how, in many cultures, money is still viewed as the root of all evil. We agree with Mark Twain's perspective: "The lack of money is the root of all evil."

Money is the fuel for a productive, world-changing existence, allowing you to innovate and direct your efforts toward your purpose. Instead of fighting for your survival, money provides the means to keep your body and mind healthy, while helping you achieve the quality of life you desire.

> **Money is the fuel for a productive, world-changing existence, allowing you to innovate and direct your efforts toward your purpose.**

Interestingly, the relationship between money and happiness is more complicated than people think. When you start earning money, up to a certain level of income, happiness will almost always increase. That's because you are meeting your basic human needs, and you no longer worry whether you will eat tomorrow or how you will pay your rent next month, so you will be happier and feel more secure.

Thinking that all your happiness will come from money is a fallacy. In fact, some of the richest people in the world do not appear much happier than people with almost no money. Conny's experience, based on thirty years of meeting wealthy people, goes one step further: "Sometimes, the wealthier you are, the more unhappy you become." Still, many entrepreneurs chase the goal of becoming billionaires one day, continuing to run the race for more money.

In Conny's view, as you begin to acquire more money, your happiness will increase in certain ways. Maybe you can buy some of the things you were always dreaming about. Or perhaps you can send your children to the best schools because money no longer appears to be an issue. At the same time, you will also start to encounter problems you would not have had previously. With a certain level of wealth, your life becomes an enterprise. You now require an "infrastructure" and a constant level of liquidity to keep things going. You may easily become trapped in the system you created. Furthermore, friendship dynamics may be altered, and you will encounter new challenges with investments and taxation. More money does not necessarily mean a simpler life.

For many of us, the main motivation for acquiring wealth is to make life better for the next generation. You want your kids to live better than you did. At the same time, we have seen that children who inherit large amounts of money are seldom well-equipped to deal with it. The biggest gift you can give to your children is your own financial security and modelling the best mindsets around money. There is nothing wrong with wanting more money, as long as you are clear about your motivations.

Like with failure, Europeans seem to struggle with money itself, especially talking about it. In fact, a German proverb says, "Mention money and the whole world is silent." If you, like us, grew up in a society or environment that doesn't talk openly about money, you shouldn't be surprised that you are not equipped to deal with it. And you certainly should not be shocked if you feel like you are doing something wrong by wanting more money. You may even feel guilty if you make a lot of money. It is not like this everywhere, though. In other parts of the world, like the U.S. or China, making a lot of money is highly desirable and often a primary goal.

Walid Abboud, a successful entrepreneur and serial investor, discusses these differences in perceptions. He says, "Not wanting to speak about money is a European luxury. Here, people know there's a government that can take care of them, that's going to pay for their school, or the school of their kids, that there is a health system they can access, and that there are unemployment benefits available. It is easy to say, 'I don't want to speak about money,' when such basic needs are secured. The fact that growing up in certain cultures, speaking about money was a taboo, has led to the financial illiteracy we are confronted with today."

> **We must educate our children about money management and engage in open conversations about everything money can bring to your life, both good and bad.**

Considering the increasing financial pressure governments face, and the economic disparity between social classes, we strongly believe that we need to bring this topic into the light. We must educate our children about money management and engage in open conversations about everything money can bring to your life, both good and bad. Most importantly, we must establish what financial independence or financial freedom means to each of us.

"The real measure
of your wealth
is how much
you'd be worth
if you lost
all your money."

— Bernard Meltzer

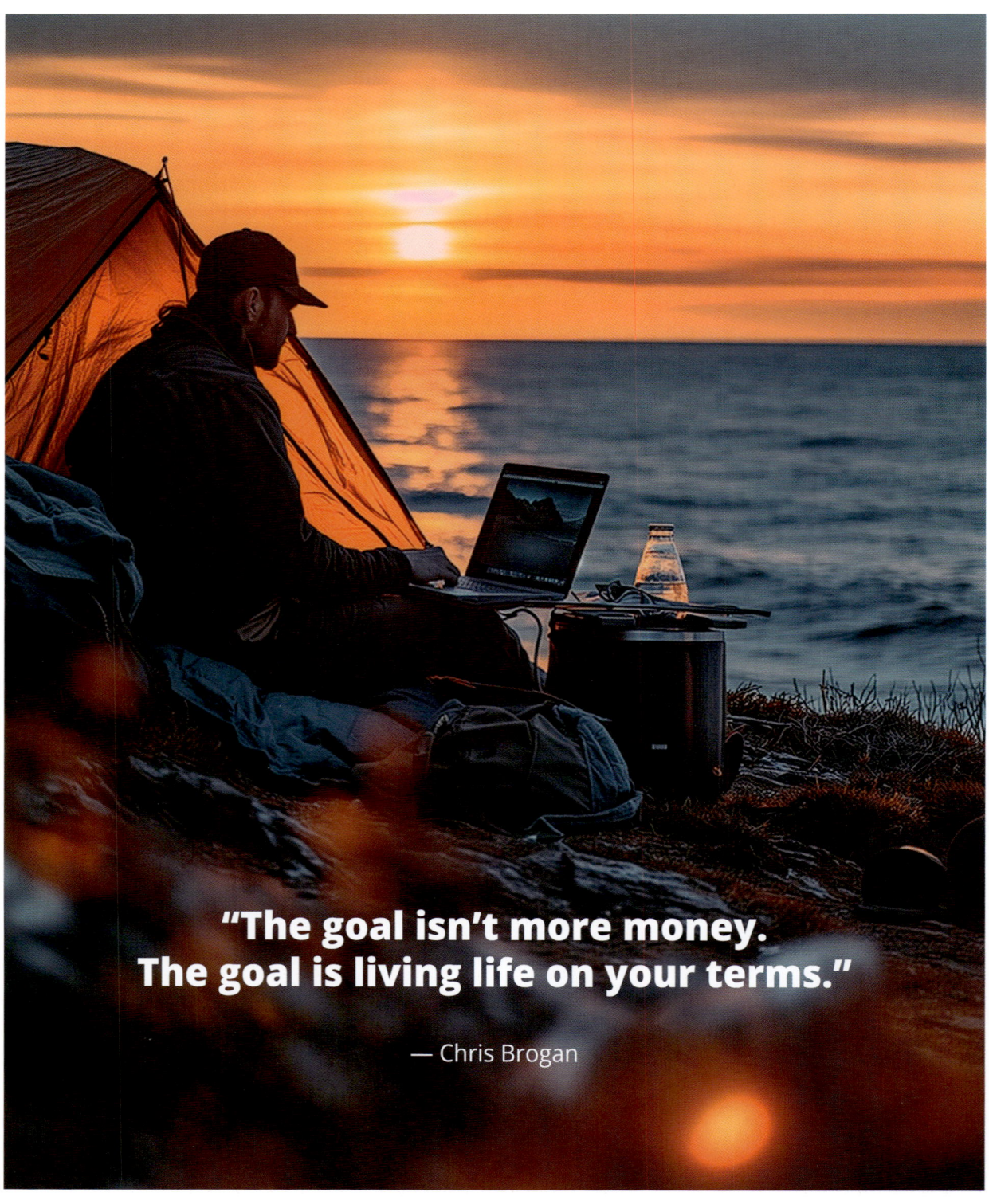

"The goal isn't more money.
The goal is living life on your terms."

— Chris Brogan

Financial Freedom: A Personal Choice

Our definition of financial freedom is simply the absence of worrying about your basic needs, whatever that means for you. It can include the money for the trips that are essential for your business success or knowing that the long-term expenditures you are committed to, like paying for the schooling for your kids or paying for the care of your parents, are financially possible.

If you worry every day about how you will pay your bills, it becomes difficult to focus on business. Experiencing financial difficulty affects your ability to operate at your best at work, it erodes your clarity and confidence, and it can put your body under a lot of stress. That shouldn't come as a surprise, considering how our sense of security and safety is affected by the lack of money. According to Abraham Maslow's pyramid of needs, safety and security belong to the basic survival levels. As a result, the pressure to meet them can take over and block us from fulfilling higher psychological needs such as love and self-actualisation. When financial responsibilities lie on your shoulders, and you feel trapped under the weight of not having enough money, there's not a lot of space left to invest in your personal growth or enjoy time with friends and family.

More money doesn't guarantee that you will be happy. Nevertheless, the absence of money can cause life to become exponentially more difficult. Financial independence makes your life easier by facilitating access to what you need. Most importantly, it gives you the freedom to do what you enjoy in life. By this, we don't mean being able to travel or attend the music or art events you enjoy. We mean the freedom to decide the work you do and the people you live with, as well as choosing the life partner you want. When you're young, financial independence also frees you from having to depend on your parents' generosity and from living your life according to their expectations.

Money Management with Eyes Wide Open

As you can see, it is not possible to have an honest 360-degree look at your life without paying attention to your finances. Be realistic and truly honest with yourself: facing your financial situation can be a great wake-up call! Even if you end up broke during certain periods of your life, it is ultimately your mindset that will help you recover and get back on track.

"I've never been poor, only broke. Being poor is a frame of mind. Being broke is a temporary situation."

— Mike Todd

You may need to sharpen your financial awareness and learn new money management skills. Trapped in a world of convenience, where online shopping is one click away and all our communication channels are flooded with sales offers, you need presence and willpower to decide what you truly need and stop spending carelessly. Subscriptions and automatic renewals hide your spending, making it extremely easy to lose track of where your money has gone.

From an abundance mindset perspective, when faced with financial challenges, it is important to focus on how you can create better financial returns. Reflecting on the financial independence and peace of mind you desire will help you focus on your business and the income you want to generate.

Ken Honda, bestselling author of *Happy Money* and one of the most recognised money coaches worldwide, talks about "Money EQ" as a reflection of your personal beliefs and thoughts about money. He stresses the importance of being aware of your emotions when you think of money, as well as how your subconscious mind makes financial decisions on autopilot.

Just like someone who neglects their emotional intelligence struggles to reach their full potential, those who neglect their Money EQ cannot be sustainably and successfully wealthy, even if they work hard and make the right investments. Through the Money EQ program he offers, Honda helps people change destructive beliefs while developing a positive attitude towards money.

"Many people take no care of their money till they come nearly to the end of it, and others do just the same with their time."

— Johann Wolfgang von Goethe

To be financially independent, you need to look ahead and plan wisely. Balance your earnings and expenditures to ensure you always end up on a positive. Walid Abboud's perspective on spending - although it might not be the thing you want to hear - is a great recipe for avoiding debt: "As an entrepreneur, the moment I started to earn money, I didn't change anything in my lifestyle. I didn't need anything special for myself, and I knew it was a pity to take money out from my company to spend it. I was happy with what I had. I'm lucky to be a person who doesn't need social recognition and always looks at the value I get for money. So, I'm not the kind of guy who is ready to pay five times more for an extra 5 per cent value, when it comes to a product or a service."

It may be tempting to spend the money you make, or overspend the moment you can "afford" high-end brands. By following Walid's advice, you will be in a much better position to avoid debt.

> **It's not about the money; it's about the emotions and energy tied to it. Your relationship with money influences your financial well-being.**

Debt

With easily accessible credit, it's possible to purchase and enjoy expensive products without immediately having to pay for them. The danger of accumulating extensive debt is therefore becoming a problem for many people. As a person (or even as a country!), reaching high levels of debt puts huge pressure on you, with detrimental effects on your health and relationships. Walid's recommendation is very clear: from the moment you have a predictable income, "you need to be strict, spend the minimum required for your basic needs, invest first, and then spend the remaining extra on nice-to-haves." This will not only keep you away from accumulating debt but will also help you generate savings to count on or enjoy when the time is right. Being ruthless when it comes to your basic expenditures will guarantee your freedom, both in a figurative and practical sense.

"Too many people spend money
they haven't earned,
to buy things they don't want,
to impress people they don't like."

— Will Rogers

Financial Freedom: The Business Perspective

"Your economic security does not lie in your job;
it lies in your own power
to produce, to think, to learn, to create, to adapt.
That's true financial independence. It's not having wealth;
it's having the power to produce wealth. It's intrinsic."

— Stephen R. Covey

One of the reasons we believe it's best to start a company while you're young is that you don't have all the liabilities that come with a settled life. If you were to start your own company right out of school or university, you would have nothing to lose, and no big cost structures yet. You wouldn't have a mortgage or school fees; you can take risks and be okay with failure and money loss. And when your business is in a growth phase, you will have the strength not to sell too early!

In Conny's opinion, selling too early is the biggest mistake entrepreneurs can make. It's a huge problem European entrepreneurs have. We want to make our first million and keep it safe in the bank. We get excited about short-term profits and overlook the long-term prospects our company may have. However, selling too early means you miss the chance to develop your company and make the most out of your idea.

When Mark Zuckerberg had the opportunity to sell Facebook, its valuation was US$1 billion. However, he declined, because he had something bigger in mind. From today's perspective, it is clear that Zuckerberg made the right call; as of December 2023, Meta (Facebook) has a market cap of US$562 billion.[1] He needed to be brave and confident in his abilities to refuse a US$1 billion offer. But so many times, when people become successful, they still operate from the basic fear of never becoming poor again. They limit their chances of achieving more, and this is one of the main reasons why the E.U. produces fewer unicorn companies compared to the United States. The mindset you have at the start can hinder you from making great decisions.

As an investor, Conny has often been asked by founders and business partners to convince their family or life partner not to sell at that early moment in time. He remembers what happened to his business partner Bernie, who was a 25 per cent shareholder in his first company, SABECO GmbH. His father told him to get "a real job" first, before taking the full risk of becoming an entrepreneur, since this "real job" would enable him to make enough money to pay for his family. Bernie ended up leaving the company they started and began working for a cheese manufacturer. Ultimately, this decision cost him DM$200 million.

Conny tells young founders he is coaching that "becoming a successful entrepreneur means falling up the stairs with bleeding knees. On the way to becoming successful and wealthy, you have many,

---

1 - "Market capitalization of Meta (Facebook) (FB)," CompaniesMarketCap, accessed January 15, 2024, https://companiesmarketcap.com/facebook/marketcap/.

many moments where it looks really bad. I tell you this from my own experience - because I rarely met anybody who was not almost bankrupt before becoming successful. It is normal to experience two or three incredibly difficult breakdowns where you truly contemplate giving up before you enjoy your final breakthrough. The essence is to overcome those moments where it's so difficult and to keep on going."

I rarely met anybody who was not almost bankrupt before becoming successful.

Based on this advice, we are going to tell you something that will sound counter-intuitive: when you start, you need to be prepared to risk your financial independence! Starting out as an entrepreneur requires a good amount of bravery, so if you're someone who worries constantly about the risks involved, then you will most likely never make it. High-risk situations are abundant in entrepreneurship; making a big decision and "failing" only presents you with an opportunity to learn. If you truly want to succeed, there is no other way than to take leaps of faith and develop incredible courage.

It is very important to be honest with yourself about how well you can handle uncertainty and financial insecurity, both personally and as a business owner. Starting a company is often a trade-off. If you go into the corporate world, you will quickly receive a steady, dependable income that you can spend to make money quicker and not limit yourself when travelling or buying things in the prime time of your life. The compromise you need to make as an entrepreneur is to give up short-term gains in favour of long-term wealth.

From Conny's experience of investing in more than 400 companies, most companies take ten or more years to succeed. Even online businesses with low start-up costs need four to eight years to find out if they can succeed. Very rarely has he encountered people who became successful in more quickly than this. Yes, we read about and admire these "lighthouse entrepreneurs." But they are the rare exceptions and not the norm for most founders.

Risk, Revisited

"I believe that through knowledge and discipline, financial peace is possible for all of us."

— Dave Ramsey

We mentioned earlier in the book that many people are so risk-averse that they may try to convince you to take the "safe" route in life, rather than pursuing entrepreneurship. As a result, most people choose a 9-to-5 job instead of pursuing an exciting (yet unpredictable) adventure. These so-called "safe" jobs and "guarantees" of lifetime employment with big companies, however, are now a myth; jobs for life no longer exist. While jobs for life may have existed fifty years ago, that is no longer the case. In fact, mass layoffs have become so common at large corporate companies that the "normal" 9-to-5 jobs might be almost as unpredictable as an entrepreneurial career.

You need to have the courage to take risks throughout your entire entrepreneurial life. The best "risk it all" example we all know is Elon Musk, who, after selling PayPal in 2002, bet his entire payout on his next business venture, SpaceX. There wasn't much of a market for spaceships at the time, and no customers were fighting to buy the product. Despite that, he believed the market would establish itself in time, and he ended up becoming the richest man on the planet in 2021.

When asked about building Tesla and SpaceX, Musk acknowledged that it was "rewarding but massively difficult . . ." His secret to becoming so wealthy was that he didn't sell the stock in the companies. His belief confirms the advice we gave before about not selling too early: "You shouldn't take money off the table - or stock off the table . . . [and] a captain should go down with their ship." Obviously, this mindset paid off for him!

Don't Let Money Be Your Why!

Another important piece of advice that your accountant, CFO, or stakeholders might disagree with is to never chase money. If you chase money, it will actually "run away" from you. Very few successful entrepreneurs' main aim is to become rich. Rather, there is a direct correlation between the reasons behind the business and the odds that the business will succeed. Most people who say they want to become rich - and make it their only focus - do not succeed. On the other hand, the ones wanting to serve a particular customer or market in a better way have a much higher chance of success.

If you chase money, it will actually "run away" from you.

Making money is the side product of accomplishing something or adding value to whatever work you do. As an entrepreneur, you either want to solve a problem or respond to one of your clients' needs. So, when you do your life planning, focus on becoming a successful entrepreneur, not only on becoming rich - because that will bring much more richness to your life than the money you are making.

Always Remember to Live a Rich Life

To become successful and financially independent is one of the greatest feelings an entrepreneur can experience! Financial independence is very difficult to achieve, and it can change your behaviour. When Conny sold his first company, it took him many years to realise that he was rich. This relates to the last piece of "financial advice" to offer you: don't let money prevent you from living a rich life.

Consider this: we experience money differently at different ages. There may be a time when all you want is your first Porsche, and then, like many young entrepreneurs who land their first big paycheck, you may eventually buy it. You might even buy a second one; this is what Conny did - until he began asking himself, "Do I need a Porsche anymore?" Because all these material things don't genuinely result in a rich life. They are only material, so it's important to keep a balance.

As you spend money, do not become a slave to your possessions. Know your value so you do not feel that you need to prove your worth with the latest car, watch, or destination holiday. Remember, we only have one life - and it is not solely defined by our bank accounts.

"If money is your hope for independence, you will never have it.
The only real security that a man will have in this world
is a reserve of knowledge, experience, and ability."

— Henry Ford

For Walid, when he started as an entrepreneur thirty years ago, money was a real need to solve his family's debt. "How we relate to money will evolve throughout our life. Now, the most precious thing money gives me is time. When you can afford to spend money to make your life easier, you gain invaluable time you can invest in what's most important for you - your family, your growth."

Our life span is limited, so when it comes to spending, consider your income and expenses while developing a buffer of security . . . and then commit to living the life you want - taking the business risks which your gut tells you to go for.

We view financial independence as not relying on someone else to cover your expenses, and financial freedom as a mindset that allows you to live the life you've always wanted. Financial independence as a goal is simply a number - and it's possible that when you achieve it, you may still not be happy. Financial freedom, on the other hand, means starting to live the life that you want to live, and it is achievable well before you reach financial independence.

Finding Freedom through Your Vision

Before starting to reflect on your own vision of financial independence, take a moment to recognise and address anything that may be holding you back from becoming financially independent. Maybe you are influenced by old beliefs, like thinking that having lots of money makes you a bad person. Or, perhaps there's a deep loyalty to your family, and you're hesitant to outshine their achievements. Reflect on whether a lack of self-confidence or a belief that you don't truly deserve financial success might be playing a role. By acknowledging and putting words to these thoughts, you're taking the first step towards rewriting your story. Replace any limiting beliefs with affirmations that resonate with your vision for financial freedom, creating an empowering narrative that supports your vision.

Conny's vision is to "have the financial freedom to enjoy life and work throughout my entire existence, and to offer my dear ones the security they need." However, your vision may be very different.

When we asked Walid about his vision, he shared, "For me, being financially independent means having a recurring revenue. I wouldn't get a sense of being financially secure, or even rich, if you would simply give me a large amount of money. Even if you give me a billion dollars, I wouldn't feel rich or very comfortable. My vision is to have a recurring income that is double the amount required to maintain my quality of life and remain the protector of my extended family."

As you reflect on the questions above, consider what will motivate you to achieve your financial vision. It might be your peace of mind so you can focus on your business, or it might be having more time to enjoy with the people you love. You may want to consider how financial freedom will change the lives of your loved ones as well. By calling to mind these "incentives," you are much more likely to remain motivated, even in the face of challenges.

Writing this book, we increasingly realised that our individual financial independence is not related to material things only. There are many important things in our life for which we would be happy to reduce our standard of living without regret.

LET'S REVIEW

In this chapter, you learned how to create your definition of financial freedom that transcends a monetary goal. Financial freedom allows you to focus not just on the money you are making but also on the motivation behind your business. You've learned that it's critical to balance making money, spending it, and saving it to enjoy your life now—and not just when you make a certain wealth.

Limiting beliefs, the temptation to sell too soon, making purchases before you are financially secure, and the well-intentioned, conservative advice from friends and family are pitfalls to avoid in designing the life of your dreams. Instead, maintain a clear vision for your version of financial independence - and work diligently toward that goal. Stay on course, and you will enjoy the journey of entrepreneurship as you get closer to financial independence and freedom.

WHAT'S NEXT

No matter how much money you make, enjoying financial independence can be extremely difficult if your health is compromised—or if you have other physical limitations that prevent you from fully enjoying the money you have. Therefore, it's time to delve into the topic of physical wellness, because without maintaining peak physical condition, you may not be able to fully enjoy all the positive people, places, and things that you are calling into your life.

CHAPTER SIX

Body Health and Fitness:
Nurturing Your Physical Vitality

"The human body is the best work of art."

— Jess C. Scott

FROM FOOTBALL TO FIT FOR LIFE

When I was young, I had a dream: to become a professional football player. I was talented at football, as well as track and field, and I knew that, with enough practice, I had the potential to achieve this dream. My hopes were dashed, however, when I was told my chances of being injured were statistically higher than what was accepted at a professional level, "thanks" to my body constitution. From that moment on, I stopped playing sports for pleasure. Eventually, I started going to the gym, because I realised that if I didn't work out regularly, I would gain weight, lose muscle, and I would generally feel uncomfortable in my body.

When you are young, your body can better tolerate eating less healthy foods and drinking more alcohol - plus, it's easier to function with less sleep. By the age of forty, I suddenly noticed a metabolism change and started wondering why the muscles on my belly were less visible, even if I reduced my food intake. Gone were those teenage years of having a six-pack, even without working out!

Today, at the age of fifty-five, my vision is to have a healthy, fit, attractive body. I also want to wake up feeling energised every morning, ready for success. This vision has become my go-to when I make decisions about what and how I eat, when and where I sleep, and the kind of exercise that I am doing.

I strongly believe that if I am not healthy, nothing else matters. The motivation to take good care of my body is to be able to enjoy a long life and be in excellent physical shape in later years - as well as feel confident when I look in the mirror. I also have another very powerful motivation for exercising: stress relief! Going to the gym after work helps me "digest" what happened during the day.

Simply spending time at the gym is not enough when it comes to physical benefits. Even though I was working out four to five times a week, I wasn't gaining muscles like I should have, considering the amount of effort I was putting in. Eventually, I realised that because I avoided exercises I disliked, I was preventing myself from enjoying the full benefits I was seeking. I know that the answer to my problem would be to work with a personal trainer; not only are they experts in physical fitness but they can also be accountability partners, and this would make all the difference!

When it comes to what will work best for you, it is important to find something you enjoy; otherwise, the chances of sticking to an exercise regimen are lower. We are all different, so it's important to find something you are willing integrate into your daily routine.

As we were writing this book, I realised that, while I got regular health checks, engaged in good eating habits, and exercised consistently, I was unconsciously sabotaging my health with very poor sleep habits. This started in my forties, when sleep was not a given anymore, especially in moments when I was under a lot of stress.

If I don't have a good night's sleep, the start of the day will always be difficult. It feels awful waking up throughout the night and then struggling to focus the next day. When I made the connection between sleep and performance, I finally decided to take action to fix this; I knew it was possible, because I still sleep like a teenager when I stay at the Lanserhof Clinic, where I do not drink alcohol. When I am there, I also fast (or eat very little), eat dinner early, and significantly reduce time on the phone or tablet.

When I returned home from the clinic, I committed to monitoring my sleep habits and going to bed no later than 11:00 p.m. In addition, I decided to reduce my alcohol consumption to one glass of wine at dinner and replace the post-gym beer I was enjoying with a non-alcoholic one, knowing the positive impact this would have on the quality of my sleep. I found that, when these habits are in place, I feel unstoppable - better than I did when I was half my age!

Throughout my life, I observed how many entrepreneurs, including myself, tend to neglect their health. The fear of not succeeding often leads to prioritising work at the expense of health and well-being. We become so business-focused that other aspects of life, like physical health, take a backseat.

During moments of uncertainty, it becomes crucial to re-evaluate priorities and ensure that they are aligned with your long-term well-being and success. Ask yourself, "Am I investing my time and energy in the right areas?" And never let your physical health and fitness drop out from the top priorities!

— *Conny*

146

THE TIME IS NOW

*"Without health, life is not life; it is only a state
of languor and suffering - an image of death."*

— Buddha

We tend to take our health for granted . . . and only start appreciating it when we get sick: everything else loses importance when we are faced with a health scare. When we're young, our bodies can cope with loads of stress and neglect and still recover quickly. This leads many young people to think they don't need to worry about their health - that it will all work out. But the sooner we start taking care of our health, the better; no one wants to wake up to reality when the damage you've done to your health is irreversible.

As entrepreneurs, we often think the day is not long enough for all the things we want to do. When you're running an international business, this becomes even more acute; you're faced with the reality that the world never sleeps, so you feel the need to always be active and available. The more passion you have for your work, the easier it is to lose track of time, and you may find yourself working twelve hours per day without any discomfort. All of this would be fine if only our energy were infinite and our bodies indestructible. Unfortunately, we are vulnerable - so we do need to pay attention to how our body is coping with such demands.

Unless you are healthy, you cannot work at peak capacity to grow the business that is so important to you, and you won't be able to enjoy life's special moments either. The truth is, your body and mind are your most precious

Your body is your temple: the container of all thoughts, feelings, and experiences you will have in this life.

resources! Your body is your temple: the container of all thoughts, feelings, and experiences you will have in this life. Respect, nurture, and strengthen it, and you will live gracefully. Take it for granted, stretch it to the max, deprive it of the essential elements, and you will end up with a health crisis sooner rather than later.

Regula Curti, founder of Seeschau - House of Sacred Arts and of Beyond Foundation and Beyond Music, and businesswoman, summarised these ideas brilliantly: "Everything happens through my body. And as long as I'm on this planet, if I have a healthy body, it is a good companion to my mind and a good companion to my psyche. If my body is not healthy, it affects not only my mind but negatively impacts my quality of life, my work, and my relationships. It's key to have a healthy, functioning body; otherwise, it will always be an obstacle in everything you do. My health even affects my happiness, my impact on those around me, and how I give myself to the world . . . because I give myself to the world through my physical body."

We are often so focused on our professional success and legacy that we neglect the basic needs of our body: healthy food, water, sleep, clean air, and movement. Many times, this work trance is only interrupted by a health crisis. As an entrepreneur, you become the biggest liability to your business, if you do not take care of your body and have the energy you need to think, create, and engage with others. It's important to remind yourself that you brought that company to life, and your ideas and actions inspire partners, employees, and investors. It's your responsibility to take care of yourself first. So, with the same focus that you take care of your assets or your team, you must pay attention to preserving your health and your body - and there's no better time to start doing it than now.

When we were writing this chapter, we decided it was important to include not only the basic, commonly accepted guidelines for having a healthy and fit body but also the recent advancements when it comes to longevity. We strongly encourage you to pay attention to these recommendations, too, even if you are in your twenties or thirties.

Getting the Facts Straight

The World Health Organization's (WHO) definition of health gives us a good understanding of the factors that come into play when we are setting the foundation for optimal health and wellness: "Health is a state of complete mental, social and physical well-being, not merely the absence of disease or infirmity."[1]

This reminds us of the myriad of interdependencies between all areas of your life; we cannot approach any area in isolation. Therefore, to live life to its fullest, you must give attention to all areas. It is scientifically proven that our thoughts and the language we use in communicating with others

To live life to its fullest, you must pay attention to all its areas!

and ourselves affect our mental state and our performance. Also, if you continuously experience high levels of negative emotions, they might impact your mental and physical health, as well as the quality of your relationships. As you can see, everything we discuss in this book is interrelated and can affect your health and happiness.

So, let's begin by unpacking the essential ingredients for a healthy and fit body:
- *nutrition,*
- *sleep,*
- *exercise.*

---

1 - World Health Organization (WHO), "Constitution," accessed January 21, 2024, https://www.who.int/about/accountability/governance/constitution.

"**Wellness is the complete integration of body, mind, and spirit - the realization that everything we do, think, feel, and believe has an effect on our state of well-being.**"

— Greg Anderson

Healthy Nutrition

*"The food you eat can be either
the safest and most powerful form of medicine
or the slowest form of poison."*

— Ann Wigmore

The commonly used phrase "you are what you eat" has so much truth. The nutrients we consume, coupled with our lifestyle, are known to influence not only our health but also how we feel and our ability to live the life we want.

For example, a diet rich in fruits, vegetables, whole grains, and healthy fats (typical of the Mediterranean style of eating) has been associated with numerous health benefits. In fact, Mediterranean eating habits earned the title of best overall diet, in the 2023 rankings by *U.S. News and World Report*.[1] Meals from the sunny Mediterranean also ranked first in the categories of best diet for healthy eating and best plant-based diet.

There is no "one-size-fits-all" miracle diet, because each person's nutritional needs and responses to a certain diet can vary significantly.

Studies have found that this dietary eating style can reduce the risk of chronic diseases such as cardiovascular disease, type 2 diabetes,[2] and certain cancers, while promoting longevity and improving quality of life. Additionally, specific nutrients like omega-3 fatty acids found in fish have been linked to improved cognitive function and mood regulation. Moreover, gut health, influenced by the types of foods we eat, has emerged as a critical factor in mental health. The gut-brain connection reveals how the food we consume can impact our mood and emotions.

The Mediterranean diet is just one example of an optimal diet. There are many other scientifically backed and easy-to-access nutritional guidelines out there, too. However, there is no "one-size-fits-all" miracle diet, because each person's nutritional needs and responses to a certain diet can vary significantly.

---

1 - World Health Organization (WHO), "Constitution," accessed January 21, 2024, https://www.who.int/about/accountability/governance/constitution.
2 - Castaneda, Ruben, Medaris Miller, Anna, "A Patient's Guide to Type 2 Diabetes," *U.S. News & World Report*, August 5, 2019, https://health.usnews.com/conditions/diabetes/type-2-diabetes.

Blood Sugar and Cholesterol

Regardless of the diet that works for you, one important thing to keep in mind when we talk about nutrition is sugar. Dr Andreas Brauchlin, a specialist in cardiology and internal medicine and medical director of the Swiss Medical Centre, states that regulating and maintaining stable blood sugar levels is crucial for overall health, effective weight management, and longevity: "Fluctuations in blood sugar can lead to various health issues, such as diabetes, heart disease, and inflammation. Stable blood sugar levels play a significant role in weight management as well. When blood sugar spikes, the body tends to release more insulin, which can lead to fat storage. At the same, the high peak of insulin will lower the blood sugar levels in short time, and this drop of blood sugar then can trigger hunger and cravings again shortly after eating, a phenomenon we often see in "junk food" and other unhealthy foods with "quick sugars". By regulating blood sugar smoothly with "healthy" high quality food, slowly metabolized, you can better control your appetite, make healthier food choices, and maintain a healthier weight." Chronically high blood sugar levels can accelerate aging at a cellular level and increase oxidative stress, contributing to premature aging and a shorter lifespan.

Dr Andreas Brauchlin further explains that regulating and maintaining stable blood sugar levels through diet involves choosing wholegrain, unprocessed foods, prioritising high-fibre options, and avoiding refined carbohydrates and sugary beverages. Including protein and unsaturated fats with each meal, controlling portion sizes, and staying hydrated also contribute to stable blood sugar levels.

Since individual responses to different foods can vary, it's essential to listen to your body and monitor how different foods affect your blood sugar levels. Consulting with a dietitian can also provide personalised guidance and support you in managing your blood sugar through diet.

Cholesterol also plays an important role in nutrition because it is a crucial component of cell membranes and is necessary for the synthesis of hormones, bile acids, and vitamin D. However, excessive levels of cholesterol, particularly low-density lipoprotein (LDL) cholesterol (also known as "bad" cholesterol), can contribute to the development of cardiovascular diseases.

Scientifically based, practical recommendations for managing cholesterol levels include adopting a balanced, heart-healthy diet, such as the aforementioned Mediterranean diet. Limiting the consumption of processed and fried foods that contain trans fats is essential as well, since trans fats raise LDL cholesterol levels and increase the risk of heart disease.

At the age of twenty-five, Conny began scheduling annual visits at a holistic clinic - like the Max Grundig Klinik in the Black Forest and Lanserhof in Lans or at Lake Tegernsee - for a general medical check-up and nutritional support. In Lanserhof, he noticed the positive effects of fasting in particular, which has scientifically proven health benefits and supports longevity as well.

Some of the benefits of fasting include improved metabolic health, weight loss, enhanced brain function, increased insulin sensitivity, and reduced inflammation. Fasting can also promote autophagy, which is the body's process of removing damaged cells. It may have potential benefits in promoting longevity and disease prevention. Some studies even suggest that intermittent fasting can aid in cardiovascular health and support a healthier gut microbiome. But before starting, it's essential to approach fasting with caution and consult a healthcare professional, especially if you have any underlying health conditions or concerns.[1]

---

1 - *The New England Journal of Medicine* in December 2019.3; Pelz, Mindy, *Fast Like a Girl: A Woman's Guide to Using the Healing Power of Fasting to Burn Fat, Boost Energy, and Balance*, Hay House Inc., December 27, 2022; *The Journal of Nutrition, Health & Aging* in 2018.

Next-Level Nutrition

"There are many ways to love your body. But fuelling your body with nutritious food is the highest form of self-respect."

— Ania Drosnes

If you want to take your nutrition to the next level, you need to be guided by the three universal principles highlighted by Dr Mark Hyman, an authority in the functional medicine space: focus on quality, make "food as medicine" the guiding principle for everything you eat, and personalise your diet to fit your metabolism, genetics, and preferences.

Dr Hyman is a firm believer that food is the most powerful drug on the planet, having the power to not only prevent disease but to reverse it: "What you put on your fork is more powerful than anything you find at the bottom of your prescription." His books, such as *The 10-Day Detox Diet, Food: What the Heck Should I Eat, Food Fix,* to *Young Forever* - as well as his podcast, "The Doctor's Pharmacy" - are amazing resources you can turn to.

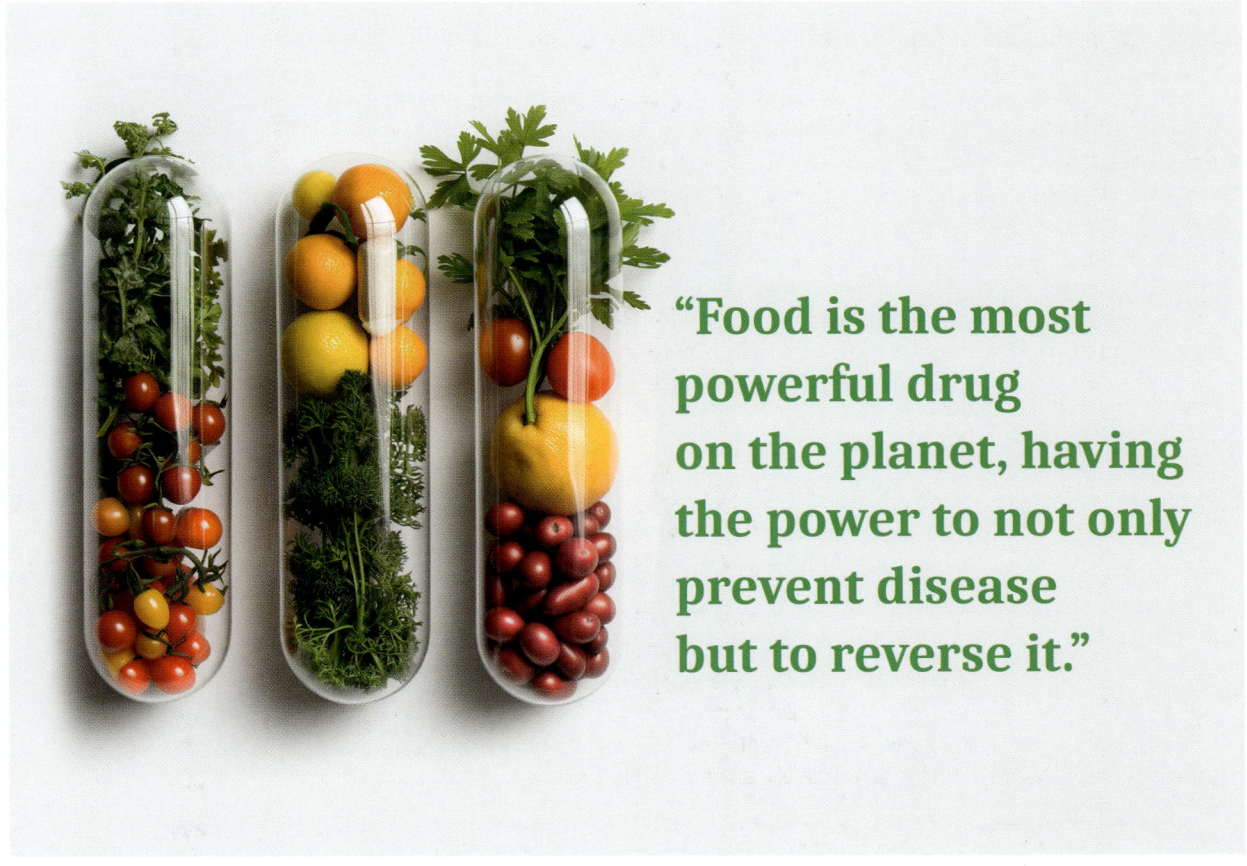

"Food is the most powerful drug on the planet, having the power to not only prevent disease but to reverse it."

A discussion of nutrition in the twenty-first century would not be complete without touching on the topic of nutritional biohacking. Nutrition biohacking involves the strategic use of personalised dietary approaches and lifestyle modifications to optimise health, performance, and well-being. By leveraging scientific knowledge and technology, individuals fine-tune their nutritional intake to achieve specific goals, such as improving energy levels, enhancing cognitive function, managing weight, or supporting athletic performance. This emerging field emphasises that each person's nutritional needs and responses can vary significantly. Nutrition biohacking encourages experimentation, self-monitoring, and data-driven decision-making to unlock the potential of one's body and mind, leading to a more empowered and proactive approach to personal health and vitality.

Alcohol

The WHO refers to alcohol as a "toxic and psychoactive substance with dependence-producing properties."[1] However, a glass of wine or a beer might be a regular occurrence in our daily lives. We drink to unwind, relax, increase our self-esteem, or even indirectly deal with a problem. But alcohol is a depressant that affects the central nervous system, impacting the way we think, act, and feel.

For many years, health officials have said that moderate drinking (defined as up to a drink per day for women and up to two per day for men)[2] won't do any damage to the body and may even offer some health benefits. This "conventional wisdom" is changing rapidly, however, as more and more research emerges, revealing the harmful effects of even a small amount of alcohol on our body, brain, and health.

You can gain a comprehensive overview of the impact of alcohol by listening to Andrew Huberman, professor of neurobiology at Stanford School of Medicine who, in his podcast "The Huberman Lab," shares brand new scientific findings from the most reputable scientists of our time. He recently discussed the physiological effects that drinking alcohol has on the brain and body over time and at different levels of consumption.[3]

The prestigious *Lancet* journal also tackles the issue, with a new paper in which Emmanuela Gakidou, professor of global health and health metrics sciences at the University of Washington, states: "The evidence is adding up that no amount of drinking is safe," based on a review of nearly 700 existing studies on global drinking prevalence and nearly 600 studies on alcohol and health.[4]

You may still decide to drink a glass of alcohol from time to time. Being aware of how alcohol affects you physically and psychologically, however, you may be more motivated to drink in moderation and stay conscious of your alcohol consumption.

The bottom line about nutrition? There is no perfect recipe applicable to all of us, as we need to tailor our approach to many factors like age, metabolism, lifestyle, medications, and existing health concerns. One thing is sure: wisely choosing what, how, when, and how much we eat and drink can make a difference in nearly every aspect of our lives.

---

1 - World Health Organization, "Alcohol," Accessed January 21, 2024, https://www.who.int/health-topics/alcohol#tab=tab_1.
2 - Ducharme, Jamie, "A New Study Says Any Amount of Drinking Is Bad for You. Here's What Experts Say," *Time*, August 24, 2018, https://time.com/5376552/how-much-alcohol-to-drink-study/.
3 - Huberman, Andrew, "What Alcohol Does to Your Body, Brain & Health," Huberman Lab, notes, August 21, 2022, https://hubermanlab.com/what-alcohol-does-to-your-body-brain-health/.
4 - Griswold, Max, Fullman, Nancy, Hawley, Caitlin, Arian, Nicholas, et al, "Alcohol Use and Burden for 195 Countries and Territories, 1990–2016: A Systematic Analysis for the Global Burden of Disease Study 2016," *Lancet* 392 (10152): 1015–35, https://www.thelancet.com/article/S0140-6736(18)31310-2/fulltext.

Sleep

"Best nootropic: sleep. Best stress relief: sleep. Best trauma release: sleep. Best immune booster: sleep. Best hormone augmentation: sleep. Best emotional stabilizer: sleep."

— Dr Andrew D. Huberman

Most of us have heard that we need seven to nine hours of sleep every night.[1] But we simply ignore it, not taking seriously the importance of sleep for our body and mental health. For decades, we have been worshipping the myth of the super-achiever: someone who works and plays hard, operating with no more than five hours of sleep per night. This was the façade successful Wall Street billionaires portrayed to the world. As a result, generations of corporate America employees, from CEOs to interns, aiming to reach that level of success, were making sleep deprivation a badge of honour and an unspoken agreement at the start of any job.

After collapsing on the floor of her home office in 2007 due to exhaustion and lack of sleep, Arianna Huffington, co-founder and editor-in-chief of *Huffington Post* at the time, became a true "sleep evangelist." In her book, *Thrive*, she reminds us, "There is a reason why sleep deprivation is classified as a form of torture and is a common strategy employed by religious cults. They force prospective members to stay awake for extended periods to reduce their subject's decision-making ability." She urges us to "ignore the workaholic wisdom that says we're lazy for not living up to the example set by notorious self-professed undersleepers. Each of us is more likely to be a professional powerhouse if we're not asleep at the wheel." In 2017, with her book *Sleep Revolution*, she boldly (and humorously) called for high achievers to "sleep their way to the top."

Matthew Walker, PhD, professor of neuroscience and psychology at the University of California, Berkeley, synthesises decades of clinical practice and research in his New York Times and international bestseller, *Why We Sleep*, making scientifically proven arguments for the importance of sleep.

Walker highlights the benefits of sleep for the brain, especially for our memory and creativity, stressing the importance of at least seven hours of sleep each night (for most people) to maintain our cognitive performance and ability to concentrate. Sharing the outcome of more than twenty large-scale epidemiological studies that have tracked millions of people over decades, he summarises the research in simple terms: "The shorter your sleep, the shorter your life."

Heart disease, obesity, dementia, diabetes, and cancer all have a causality linked to lack of sleep. It is not only about the quantity but also the quality of sleep, he notes. Walker dedicates one chapter to the importance of dreaming as an overnight therapy, sharing breakthrough data about REM sleep: it is the only time during an entire day when your brain is completely free from anxiety-triggering molecules and can recalibrate your emotional circuits. Walker offers twelve recommendations for improving your sleep, which we have provided below (adapted from his website):

---

1 - National Health Service, "Insomnia," Last modified March 12, 2021, https://www.nhs.uk/conditions/insomnia/.

12 TIPS FOR GOOD SLEEP

1 **Stick to a schedule.**
Go to bed and wake up at the same time each day; if necessary, set an alarm for bedtime.

2 **Don't exercise too late in the day**
If you do exercise in the afternoon or evening, ensure you exercise least two to three hours before going to bed, so your nervous system has time to wind down.

3 **Avoid caffeine and nicotine.**
Consuming food and drinks that contain stimulants (colas, coffee, teas that aren't herbal, chocolate) in the afternoon can have a negative influence on your sleep.

4 **Avoid alcoholic drinks before bed.**
Having a drink before bed can help you relax and fall asleep, but you won't sleep as deeply or as long before waking up.

5 **Avoid large meals and beverages late at night.**
Instead, have a light snack before bed, as heavy meals can cause digestive issues, and interfere with sleep. Drinking too many fluids can cause frequent awakenings to urinate.

6 **Avoid medicines that delay or disrupt your sleep (when possible).**
If you currently take a medication that may be affecting your sleep (prescription, over-the-counter, herbal, medicines) discuss potential options with your healthcare provider.

7 **Don't nap after 3:00 p.m.**

8 **Make sure to leave time to relax before bed.**
Give yourself some time before going to bed to unwind after a stressful day, to get your body and mind into a more calm, relaxed state.

9 **Take a warm bath before bed.**
The drop in body temperature after a bath may help you to feel sleepy, as it slows you down and relaxes you before bed.

10 **Maintain a dark, cool (temperature-wise), gadget-free bedroom.**
The temperature in the room should be kept on the cool side ($18\ ^0C$). From 9 p.m. onwards, reduce blue light to increase your melatonin level and prepare for sleep. Ideally keep mobile phones and computers out of your bedroom.

11 **Get adequate amounts of sunlight exposure.**
Try to get outside in the natural sunlight for at least thirty minutes per day early in the morning to trigger the release of sleep hormones.

12 **Don't stay in bed if you (really) can't sleep.**
If you're still awake after more than twenty minutes, or you start to get anxious in bed, get up and do something else until you feel sleepy.

Besides Matthew Walker's books, we highly recommend you check his Masterclass course, the Insomnia podcast, and the rich resources available on sleepfoundation.org. Not only will you get a full view of the importance of sleep, but you will also acquire some excellent tools and techniques to harness it.

Sleep impacts nearly every aspect of your life. If you want to find out more about sleep, an additional resource is *Life Time*, written by Russel Foster, PhD, professor of circadian neuroscience at Oxford University and founder and director of the Sleep and Circadian Neuroscience Institute. In his book, he explains the new science of the body clock, as well as how it can revolutionise your sleep and health.

Getting the appropriate amount and quality of sleep is not only beneficial to your life but imperative. If you want to slow the effects of ageing, strengthen your immune system, relieve stress, lift your mood, enhance your ability to learn, and boost your efficiency and productivity, then getting a good night's sleep every day is a very powerful and free tool. It will dramatically improve the quality of your life.

Physical Activity

*"Movement is a medicine for creating change
in a person's physical, emotional, and mental states."*

— Carol Welch

When it comes to physical exercise, we can all be inspired by Conny's father, who, at the age of ninety, still dedicates two to three hours per day to his health. He is even jogging daily! When he was thirty, Conny's father discovered he had high cholesterol. Since then, he has committed to going into the forest daily to run or do some exercises. By focusing on his health and exercising, Conny's father beat the negative health predictions given earlier in his life due to high cholesterol.

Exercise has such a tremendous positive impact on our health and well-being that the NHS (England's healthcare system) describes it as "the miracle cure we've all been waiting for." In fact, exercising lowers the risk of early death by up to 30 per cent.[1]

According to the WHO, physical activity contributes to the prevention and management of cardiovascular diseases, cancer, and diabetes, reduces symptoms of depression and anxiety,

and enhances thinking, learning, and judgment skills.[2] It is medically proven that people who exercise regularly also have a lower risk of osteoarthritis, hip fracture, dementia, and Alzheimer's disease when getting older.[3]

To highlight the importance of moving our bodies, the U.K. Department of Health and Social Care called a sedentary lifestyle "the silent killer," highlighting that it is not enough to only raise activity levels; you must also decrease the time spent sitting down. Even if you hit your weekly exercise target, your health may still be at risk if you spend the rest of the time sitting or lying down.

When we asked our friend, mediator, coach, and author, Mia Forbes Pirie, she shared: "When I feel

---

1 - National Health Service, "Benefits of Exercise," Last modified August 4, 2021, https://www.nhs.uk/live-well/exercise/exercise-health-benefits/.
2 - World Health Organization, "Physical Activity," Last modified October 5, 2022, https://www.who.int/news-room/fact-sheets/detail/physical-activity.
3 - National Health Service Inform, "Benefits of Exercise," Last modified November 30, 2022,
   https://www.nhsinform.scot/healthy-living/keeping-active/benefits-of-exercise/.

strong in my body, I feel strong emotionally and more resilient in life. My body holds the signals that can help me live better. When I decode my body's messages, I feel happier and have more energy to fulfil my purpose." That is why her vision is to "be strong and healthy to be useful" - to paraphrase Georges Hébert.

She says that her body is a vehicle for her life force. Its role is to help her fulfil her purpose. Her view is that how we relate to what happens in our bodies and lives is more important than the body itself: "The body is precious but not the main event. This does not mean we shouldn't take care of it. I want to live in my body as fully as possible."

She believes in having a strong, healthy body in which she is comfortable, and taking care of it so that she can live a full, useful, and active life. "Because the body will change, we need to adapt with it. It can be a great teacher of perseverance, humility, and empathy. What we need most of all to take care of our bodies is the ability to listen to them and to begin again, fresh, over and over, as many times as it takes - when something changes or when we fall off the proverbial wagon and get unfit."

There are numerous wearables and applications you can use as a reminder to get your body moving. Keep in mind the basic recommendations the WHO has for adults, nineteen to sixty-five years old:

- Move more and sit less! Any physical activity is better than none. Every step counts.

- Engage in at least 150 minutes (to 300 minutes) of moderate-intensity activity, or 75 minutes (to 150 minutes) of vigorous-intensity aerobic physical activity every week.

- Perform muscle-strengthening activities of moderate or greater intensity two times a week.

Let's Talk Longevity!

When Conny turned fifty, he was so sad that he didn't want to celebrate. That was the moment he realised he now had fewer days in front of him than behind him. He realised very quickly that money alone was not enough to make it work. Fortunately, we are just at the beginning of discovering the secrets to longevity. Just 2,000 years ago, the average life expectancy was somewhere between twenty and thirty years, while today, our life expectancy is so much higher! We are already grateful to live in the twenty-first century, where we keep learning more and more about optimising our health toward greater longevity.

Longevity has become a mega trend in recent years, with massive investments in the field and remarkable experts offering research-based guidance. Some of the key names we recommend following are Dr David Sinclair, professor at Harvard Medical School, known for his research on ageing and longevity; Dr Peter Attia, founder of Early Medical, focused on lengthening lifespan and simultaneously improving health span; and Dr Mark Hyman, an international leader in Functional Medicine and co-founder of Function Health.

Whether you're looking to join the centenarians club and increase your lifespan above today's world average life expectancy of 73.2 years[1], or you just want to be as healthy as you can for as long as you live, there is one thing you must understand: the time for action is now.

"To sustain longevity, you have to evolve."

— Aries Spears

In this book, we share just a few basic principles for you, hoping we spark your interest in exploring these resources further and adapting your lifestyle for longevity. Dr Peter Attia believes **the biggest failure of modern medicine ("Medicine 2.0") is that we ignore warning signs and only act when disease has taken its hold on the body.** In his book, *Outlive: The Science and Art of Longevity*, he advocates for an era of "Medicine 3.0," which requires key mindset shifts, a focus on prevention, and increasing your health span and quality of life. He invites us to be "well-informed, medically literate to a reasonable degree, [as well as] clear-eyed about your goals, and cognizant of the true nature of risk. You must be willing to change ingrained habits, accept new challenges, and venture outside of your comfort zone if necessary. You are always participating, never passive. You confront problems, even uncomfortable or scary ones, rather than ignoring them until it's too late. You have skin in the game, in a very literal sense. And you make important decisions [...] you are no longer a passenger on the ship; you are its captain."[2]

Dr Attia stresses the importance of focusing on three strategic pillars:
- Fight against cognitive decline
- Prevent the decline (and loss) of physical body functions
- Maintain emotional health

---

1 - World Health Organization, "Life Expectancy at Birth (Years)," Accessed January 21, 2024, https://www.who.int/data/gho/data/indicators/indicator-details/GHO/life-expectancy-at-birth-(years).
2 - Attia, Peter, *Outlive: The Science and Art of Longevity*, Harmony Books, March 28, 2023, pg. 35.

In Dr Attia's words, "Longevity as a concept is really only meaningful to the extent that we are defying or avoiding all these vectors of decline simultaneously. ... To retain good health as we age, but without love and friendship and purpose, is a purgatory" we would not wish to our worst enemy.

We all have incredible power to expand our lifespan - and even to function like someone twenty years younger. If you're wondering how this can be achieved, it is primarily through accessible lifestyle interventions, like the four we list below, as suggested by Dr Attia:

1. Optimise Your Exercise Routine for Longevity

"Exercise has the power to change us profoundly,
even if we're starting from zero. It gives us the ability
to pick ourselves up off the ground - literarily and figuratively -
and become stronger and more capable."

— Dr. Peter Attia

Studies have confirmed that regular exercisers live as much as a decade longer than sedentary people.[1] You not only maintain better health, but the more aerobically (cardiorespiratory) fit you are, the more energy you will have for whatever you want to do, and your physical stamina will improve.[2] Another key element to pay attention to is muscle mass, as studies show that people over fifty years old with low muscle mass are at 40 - 50 per cent greater risk of mortality than control groups.[3]

We must be committed to a lifelong strategic training program. The more active you want to be in your eighties, the more you must do right now to accomplish those goals! According to Dr Attia, there are three dimensions you should focus on when exercising for longevity:

Cardio: A combination of sustained, steady endurance work, like jogging, cycling, or swimming, with maximal aerobic effort found with high-intensity interval training type exercises.

Strength: From combining heavy weights training with nutrition and supplements to ensure you can optimise your muscle mass and bone mineral density.

Stability: Mostly ignored, stability is critical not only in allowing you to exercise but also in preventing injury. It starts with optimising your breath while exercising and continues with paying attention to the position and movement of your feet, spine, shoulders, and hands.

---

1 - *Attia, Outlive*, pg. 218
2 - *Attia, Outlive*, pg. 219
3 - *Attia, Outlive*, pg. 223

2. Optimise Your Nutrition for Longevity

"Eat food. Not too much. Mostly plants."

— Michael Pollan

In his recent book *Young Forever: The Secrets of Living Your Longest, Healthiest Life*, Dr Mark Hyman explains Michael Pollan's advice: "You need to focus on eating real food, not the ultra-processed meals we have available everywhere, avoiding products altered by modern agriculture. Don't overeat, which is easier if you choose natural, nutrient-dense food and not modified, addictive ready-made meals. Eat mostly plants, for the medicinal, life-extending phytonutrients they contain."[1]

Dr Hyman stresses that the most important thing you can do for healthy ageing is to balance your blood sugar and keep your insulin levels low and your cells insulin sensitive: "If we were to prescribe one intervention to extend life, to prevent and reverse chronic disease, it would be to dramatically reduce or eliminate sugar, and refined starch from your diet."[2] All longevity experts stress the paramount importance of high-quality protein intake, to maintain and regain muscle; ideally 1.2 to 1.5 grams per kilogram per day, adapted according to your age, health concern, and activity level.[3]

A further recommendation from longevity science is to trigger the "starvation response" with time-restricted eating (in an 8- to 12-hour window), intermittent fasts (24 - 36 hours, up to three days or a week periodically), or fast-mimicking diets (eating 800 calories per day for five days).

3. Optimise Your Sleep for Longevity

Dr Mark Hyman emphasised the fact that if you sleep less than seven hours per night, you have a 24 per cent higher risk of early death. Your deep sleep is essential for the long-term health of your brain. In older adults, superior sleep quality (having the appropriate amount of deep and REM sleep) is associated with a lower risk of mild cognitive impairment and Alzheimer's disease. Dr Peter Attia considers good sleep "a performance-enhancing drug," not only physically but cognitively.

---

1 - Hyman, Mark, *Young Forever: The Secrets to Living Your Longest, Healthiest Life*, Little, Brown Spark February 21, 2023, pg. 105.
2 - *Hyman, Young Forever*, pg. 48.
3 - *Hyman, Young Forever*, pg. 127.

We all have incredible power to extend our lifespan.

4. Optimise Your Emotional Life for Longevity

As previously touched upon, the truth is that many of us avoid acknowledging that longevity is worthless if we live a life of misery, alone and suffering. Hence, it is critically important to prioritise our emotional health—the way we regulate our emotions and manage interpersonal relationships.[1] The sooner we address our emotional health, the better our chances to avoid clinical mental health issues, like chronic anxiety or depression. A healthy emotional life will also have a positive impact on our overall health. As with our exercise and nutrition, this is a lifetime journey to embark on.

"Feeling connected and having healthy relationships with others, and with oneself, is as imperative as maintaining efficient glucose metabolism or an optimal lipoprotein profile. It is as important to get your emotional house in order, as it is to have a colonoscopy or an Lp(a) test, if not more so. It's just a lot more complicated," acknowledges Dr Attia.[2]

If your focus is to improve your lifespan and healthspan you might want to reflect on the following:

Reflection Questions:

- Which longevity optimisation would you like to focus on this year?

- What is the first step you can take, to increase your lifespan and healthspan?

Paraphrasing Regula Curti, founder of Seeschau - House of Sacred Arts and of Beyond Foundation and Beyond Music, and businesswoman, we invite you to treat your body as a temple. As Regula says, consider what would change in your life if you were to believe: "My body is the interplay of everything, so I have to take care of myself first, every day, every morning. My body is the carrier of what I do in life. If not, I'm not able to deliver my excellence. I choose to work on my excellence every morning, every day, to give the best of myself. That's the meaning of being excellent."

Reflection Questions:

- What is your level of health and fitness?

- What essential area (nutrition, your sleep, or your physical activity) needs your immediate attention to improve your health and fitness?

- What will be the cost for your health, your family, or your business if you make no changes?

Imagine yourself being healthy, fit and living a long life, full of vitality. Accept you're a work in progress, and it will be a lifetime process. Ultimately, to stay fit and healthy, you need to become clear on your motivation, have support, good resources, and stay updated with the latest information and scientific research.

---

1 - *Attia, Outlive*, pg. 389.
2 - *Attia, Outlive*, pg. 382.

LET'S REVIEW

This chapter highlights several starting points for improving your physical fitness, including focusing on proper eating habits, getting enough sleep, and committing to an exercise routine. We also shared some longevity tips to help you remain active and healthy, no matter your age!

WHAT'S NEXT

While caring for your physical body is critical, tending to your mental state is just as important! It is imperative to integrate mental and physical health holistically. In other words, fitness in both areas is necessary for your total health and well-being. For that reason, in the next chapter, you will learn more about mastering your mind, to enhance both your mental strength and resilience. You will begin to feel empowered as you come to realise that it's all in your control.

CHAPTER SEVEN

Master Your Mind:
Enhance Your Mental Strength and Resilience

*"If you want to 10x your business,
you have to 10x your mind."*

— Michael Hengl

MINDSET WINS THE DAY

As I described at the beginning of the first chapter, one of the biggest and most challenging projects I was ever involved in was the Mountain & Co. SPAC. Even though everyone involved wanted to make this transaction happen, every party had a different agenda. During this ten-month project that involved FC Barcelona, we faced obstacles at least once a week - when we thought we had reached the end of this journey. Thankfully, the entire team had such a strong desire and commitment to make the transaction work that our creativity and energy felt limitless. Whenever we were down, we motivated each other, and each team member attempted to be more creative than the next. Simply put, failure was not an option.

It was a fascinating example of the power of team spirit. This project strengthened my resilience more than ever, considering how often everything appeared bleak, with no solution (and when most people would have given up). For the first time in my business life, I struggled with my mental resilience. There were moments when I was frustrated and about to give up. But I decided to carry on. During this time, I was not capable of thinking of anything else; I would wake up with new ideas or concerns in the middle of the night. What helped me survive was staying physically active, getting rid of negative energy at the

gym every afternoon, and maintaining a secure work and home environment, even if that meant I had to make other compromises. You simply cannot fight too many battles at the same time.

The major investor in this transaction, who committed a total of many tens of millions of Euros, was a self-made multi-billionaire. I was fascinated by his skill set and ability to structure a deal, which was very much to his benefit. He was able to give everybody the impression that he couldn't care less if this deal worked out - and only seriously got involved in the project when time pressure favoured him. His ability to play the nice guy in personal interactions and the toughest guy in business negotiations was something I had never encountered before.

I came to realise that I can only win important business deals when I am mentally fit. When entering a negotiation, the other party's toughness, our level of preparation, and even the political climate are all not nearly as important as my mental state.

There is no way I could have reached the level of mental fitness necessary to close this deal without strongly believing that I am in total control and serve as the gatekeeper for every thought - both positive and negative - that I allow in my mind. In other words, I am the ultimate creator of my beliefs.

— Conny

THE MENTAL FITNESS PARADIGM: UNVEILING THE POWER WITHIN

We strongly believe that our mental health, along with a healthy emotional life, are the most underestimated areas of overall health and well-being. For this reason, we want you to ask yourself how much time you actually invest in your mental fitness. Are you aware of your negative thoughts and how they influence your business focus or relationships? Do you take proactive measures to quiet that mental chatter and allow your creativity to fully express itself? If you are like most busy people, you probably don't make the time in your day to reflect on questions like these. You will convince yourself that you cannot afford to squeeze them into your overflowing schedule. However, it is exactly in these busy, fast-paced, and stressful times that it is most important to prioritise your mental health.

Despite the progress we have seen in recent years in removing the stigma surrounding mental health issues, we rarely admit when we are anxious, overwhelmed, or sad about events in our business lives. Instead of taking time to experience the nuances of our feelings, we label every emotion as feeling "stressed out" or "tired." Then we push through it, and we bring a low-performing version of ourselves to work (and an even worse version of ourselves home in the evening). Have you ever wondered what a difference it would make for you, your business, and your family if you were to approach life with an optimal mental state every single day?

Have you ever wondered what a difference it would make for you, your business, and your family if you were to approach life with an optimal mental state every single day?

Although the medical community is focused on describing and treating mental illness, we want to highlight the importance of maintaining mental health. Andrew Huberman, professor of neurobiology at Stanford School of Medicine and host of The Huberman Lab podcast, gives the perfect definition of mental health: "A mentally healthy person [is] someone who can be in action when they need to be in action, can relax when they need to relax, can focus when they need to focus, and can sleep when they need to sleep." Sounds like a great life, doesn't it? A life in which you can accomplish a lot, nurture effective relationships with yourself and others, and remain anchored in a regulated nervous system.

However, before we can focus on solutions, we would like to provide some context about the problem we, as a society, have with mental health.

The Problem

The WHO revealed that in 2019, nearly a billion people were living with a mental disorder. In the first year of the pandemic, depression and anxiety went up by more than 25 per cent, and mental disorders are the leading cause of disability today. An estimated twelve billion workdays are lost annually due to depression and anxiety, costing the global economy nearly one trillion U.S. dollars.[1] People with severe mental health conditions live ten to twenty years less due to preventable physical conditions.[2] And the younger generation is massively impacted as well: suicide is the fourth leading cause of death among those aged fifteen to twenty-nine.[3] This makes it even more important to pay attention to your own and your children's mental health.

Burnout

Burnout is a very personal topic for Conny. Between 2008 and 2009, when he was deeply involved in the election campaign of the Liberal Party of Germany (FDP) and dealing with an overall difficult tech market at the same time, Conny experienced depression and the loss of cheerfulness for the first time in his life. Newspapers and television were attacking him left and right, and he was not used to this amount of unfair media attention. Thankfully, people in his close environment helped him to get out of the negative spiral. In the following years, he became much more sensitive to the topic. When friends or business partners showed symptoms of burnout or depression, he tried to help as much as he could. A few of the startup founders whom he helped, some of them at the unicorn level, became his best friends. Most of them changed their lives drastically after the burnout, becoming much better, healthier versions of themselves.

As burnout massively impacts our mental health, and a significant number of entrepre-

1 - "WHO and ILO Call for New Measures to Tackle Mental Health Issues at Work," World Health Organization, September 28, 2022, https://www.who.int/news/item/28-09-2022-who-and-ilo-call-for-new-measures-to-tackle-mental-health-issues-at-work.

2 - "WHO Highlights Urgent Need to Transform Mental Health and Mental Health Care," World Health Organization, June 17, 2022, https://www.who.int/news/item/17-06-2022-who-highlights-urgent-need-to-transform-mental-health-and-mental-health-care.

3 - "Mental Health," World Health Organization, 2022, https://www.who.int/health-topics/mental-health#tab=tab_1.

neurs suffer from it, you need to be aware of the indications. This will help you not only to better manage your mental well-being but also to spot someone in your team who may be drifting towards burnout.

Burnout is not yet classified as a disease but is seen as a "work-related phenomenon." According to the 11th Revision of the International Classification of Diseases (ICD-11), burnout is a syndrome resulting from chronic workplace stress that has not been successfully managed. It is characterised by three dimensions:[1]

1. Feelings of energy depletion or exhaustion.

2. Increased mental distance from one's job or feelings of negativity or cynicism related to one's job.

3. Reduced professional efficacy.

When it comes to burnout, it is very important to take proactive steps to prevent or at least interrupt that negative spiral before chronic stress results, in order not to reach stage four or five of burnout (as identified by Freudenberg in the early seventies):[2]

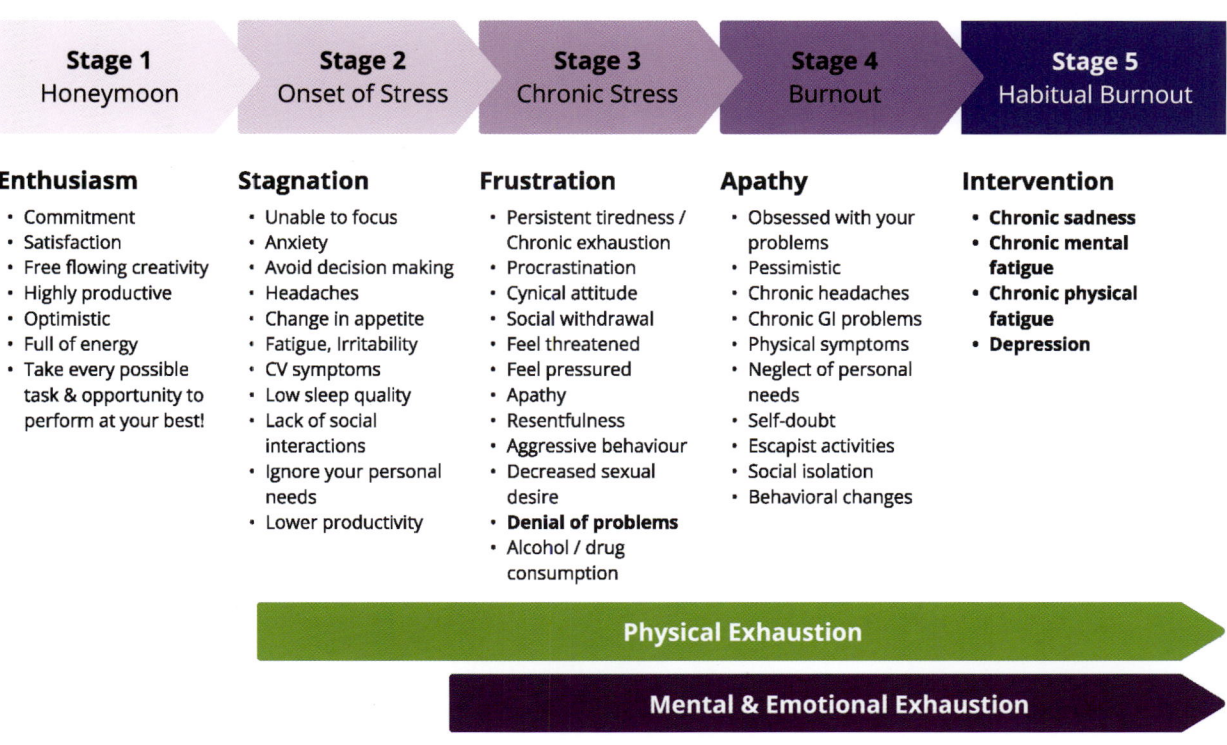

1 - "Burn-Out an 'Occupational Phenomenon': International Classification of Diseases," World Health Organization, May 28, 2019, https://www.who.int/news/item/28-05-2019-burn-out-an-occupational-phenomenon-international-classification-of-diseases.

2 - De Hert, Stefan, "Burnout in Healthcare Workers: Prevalence, Impact and Preventative Strategies," *Local and Regional Anesthesia* 13 (13): 171–83, October 28, 2020, https://www.ncbi.nlm.nih.gov/pmc/articles/PMC7604257/#cit0031.

Top tech executive Timothy Carter detailed four simple signs of burnout, emphasising the importance of taking action before it starts to have a devastating effect on you:

1. You dread going to work consistently.

2. Your mood and personality have changed (according to others).
   Trust the people around you when they say that you're more irritable, angrier, or less pleasant than you used to be.

3. You start experiencing physical symptoms (like stress headaches, insomnia, repeated "colds").

4. You always feel tired, irrespective of how much sleep you get or the amount of breaks you take from work.

Research identified predispositions for burnout in entrepreneurs who have high (idealistic) self-expectations, aim for perfection, overestimate the way they deal with challenges, feel irreplaceable, and see work as the only meaningful activity they have, which quickly becomes a substitute for their social life. If you tend to people-please, suppress your own needs, or have a strong need for recognition, you are at risk, too.

What Can You Do?

If you recognise minor symptoms of burnout, changing your lifestyle habits and optimising your work-life balance can solve the problem. In an article published in 2021 ("Burnout: A Fashionable Diagnosis" in *Deutsches Arzteblatt International*),[1] Wolfgang P. Kaschka recommends three steps:

1. Relief from stressors

2. Recuperation via relaxation and sports

3. Return to reality in terms of abandoning the ideas of perfection

Take action towards radical self-care and self-compassion, set boundaries regarding your work hours, and remove yourself from draining environments or people. Reconnect with what energises you and reframe the scenarios you have in your head, so you start seeing light within the darkness. Last but not least, ask for help when you need it!

"The reality is: there will always be more work. From our jobs and owning businesses, to being a manager of our families and our homes - there will always be more work. It never goes away. We never escape from the responsibilities that life presents us. But one of our main responsibilities should be ourselves; after all, there's only one of us anyway."

— Vanessa Autrey

---

1 - Kaschka, W. P., Korczak, D., & Broich, K, "Burnout: A Fashionable Diagnosis." *Deutsches Arzteblatt international*, 108(46), 781–787, November 18, 2011, https://pubmed.ncbi.nlm.nih.gov/22163259/.

The Ten Commandments for a Healthy & Fit Mind

Now, let's focus on the ways you can improve your mental health and fitness, through powerful techniques that have worked wonders in our lives. You don't need to apply all these strategies at once! Instead, read through the list and choose to experiment with the ideas that appeal to you.

1. Positivity

> *"The pessimist sees difficulty in every opportunity.*
> *The optimist sees the opportunity in every difficulty."*

— Winston Churchill

Winston Churchill stands as a testament to the profound impact that a single individual can have in reshaping the collective mindset of an entire nation.

Taking control of your thoughts and avoiding the fight-flight-freeze response whenever life throws a curve ball at you is a game changer! In fact, Conny has said that one of his strongest beliefs is that, when something bad happens, he views it as the start of something good! In addition, he says, "Whenever I encounter negative emotions, I limit the amount of time I dwell on those thoughts to thirty seconds. Then, I shift through my repertoire of mental tools, select the best one for the moment, and then access a positive mindset. Limiting negative thoughts helps me stay in a good flow and supports making better decisions. Plus, living this way makes you more attractive to others since everyone is drawn to a smile!

"It's far too easy, as a successful entrepreneur, to become married to your business, 24/7. And while 100 per cent commitment is necessary, this can become dangerous when the constant worries about your business start affecting your sleep, your focus, or your health.

"As an entrepreneur, something unexpected or unwanted happens nearly every single day, so it's crucial to remain calm and positive to be able to deal with it. But this can be a challenge, as it's almost fashionable to be pessimistic. It seems to have started decades ago, with that, 'Oh, don't be over-optimistic, be realistic!' Sadly, that mindset has been passed from generation to generation, dragging us down when it comes to creativity, innovation, and transformation. The Germans even have a saying, *'Ich habe schon Pferde vor der Apotheke kotzen gesehen,'* which translates to, 'I have seen horses throw up in front of the pharmacy.' It is a humorous way to express that you should always expect the worst, even when it seems impossible. While small doses of cynical humour can be entertaining, constant negativity becomes toxic and unhelpful."

"Everything begins in our mind - mind before body. We must learn to clean and master our mind in order to stay healthy in our body. The most wonderful power is the mind. It is stronger than the body."

— Regula Curti

*"A positive mind finds a way it can be done;
a negative mind looks for all the ways it can't be done."*

— Napoleon Hill

It is useless to waste precious time and energy in a negative self-blame and self-shame spiral. Even when you lose, there is a lesson to learn from it. Remind yourself that the next time you are in a similar situation, you will know how to tackle the challenge with the experience you gained. There is no such thing as bad luck. That is BS! It is all about how you look at things.

Always expect the best, because if you don't think you can win from the beginning, you've already lost. But beware: the more positive you become, the more difficult it may be to spend time and deal with cynical, critical, or pessimistic people.

*"The positive thinker sees the invisible, feels the intangible,
and achieves the impossible."*

— Winston Churchill

Knowing that our brains have difficulty differentiating between thoughts and reality, we can better understand why we should never focus too much on negative outcomes. Not only will a pessimistic perspective impact our mood and resilience, but it has a high chance of becoming a self-fulfilling prophecy. In addition to giving the negative thoughts a thirty-second time limit, you can also use a limited amount of time (perhaps ten to fifteen minutes) to write down everything you are worried or frustrated about. With this "mind detox," you don't suppress any negative emotions; instead, you offload and process them. Facing your worries and seeing them written down makes them feel more manageable and can lead to finding solutions.

Positive thinking should never be about being in denial - it is about becoming expert at living in the "possibility field" and focusing on the gain, regardless of the outcome! Being a risk-taker and an optimist will ensure that fortune favours you.

Business coach Dan Sullivan has developed the VOTA Formula to bypass our brain's tendency to notice obstacles first in order to keep us safe. This stands for vision, opposition, transformation, and action. When confronted with a difficult situation, he recommends we start by envisioning the desired outcome (being crystal clear about what we want to achieve) - the vision. Then, list everything your mind perceives as obstacles. Finally, end the cycle by transforming each of the listed oppositions into actions you need to take, decisions you will make, or communications required to surpass them. It's a simple and effective process to harness the power of negative thoughts, by shifting to solution mode![1]

In his book *Positive Intelligence: Why Only 20% of Teams and Individuals Achieve Their True Potential*

---

1 - Sullivan, Dan, "How to Harness the Power of Negative Thinking," Strategic Coach, Accessed December 31, 2023, https://resources.strategiccoach.com/the-multiplier-mindset-blog/how-to-harness-the-power-of-negative-thinking.

and How You Can Achieve Yours, Shirzad Chamine outlines that our minds are our best friends . . . and also our worst enemies at the same time. Synthesising best practices from neuroscience, organisational science, positive psychology, and co-active coaching, he introduces the Positive Intelligence Quotient (PQ). This score measures the percentage in which your mind is acting in your best interest (indicating the control you have over that part of your brain) versus that which is sabotaging you. If you want to determine your own mental fitness, you can access the PQ assessment here: https://assessment.positiveintelligence.com/pq/overview.

> *"Your potential is determined by many factors, including your cognitive intelligence (IQ), your emotional intelligence (EQ), and your skills, knowledge, experience and social network. But it's your Positive Intelligence (PQ) that determines what percentage of your vast potential you achieve."*

— Shirzad Chamine

Constantin Bisanz, serial entrepreneur and investor, who is now on a mission for more spirituality, consciousness, personal transformation, ancient wisdom, and nature conservation, gave us a different perspective on how to stop wasting so much energy with worries and doubts. "I was fascinated by the ceremony of a tribe from Brazil that we love. They start with a prayer, with no music, and very hard internal work, where all negative things are brought up and processed. Then, the second part, is singing and dancing, as they say, 'And now we give all our problems to the creator and we go to the dance floor and we enjoy life'."

2. Self-Reflection

> *"We live in a rapidly changing world, where we need to spend as much time rethinking as we do thinking. ... Changing your mind doesn't make you a flip-flopper or a hypocrite. It means you were open to learning."*

— Adam Grant

Self-reflection time should be non-negotiable. It allows you to clear your mind while asking yourself questions like: "What have I done well? What could I have done better? Where do I need to grow?" The hours that you invest in reflecting on key lessons and leaving behind negativity set the foundation for growth and success. Every now and then, you might tackle bigger questions like: "What do I really want in my life? Are there any changes I could make to be become better, not just financially, but also in my relationships with the people I care about? Do I live a life true to myself or the life others expect of me?"

Conny likes to write down what he has achieved at the end of every day, so when he does an end-of-the-year review, he won't be influenced by recent negative incidents but instead will have a balanced picture that focuses on the positives. He says, "In the past twenty-five years, I have never ended a year with a heavy heart or sense of failure."

This simple practice - choosing what you want to focus on at the end of every year - builds confidence and mental strength, generating good feelings and gratitude for what life is offering, both big and small.

Georg Graf von Walderdorff, entrepreneur and business angel, highlights: "Entrepreneurs need time and inner peace, to reflect. I put one hour of 'me-time' in my diary every day. This slot is reserved for reflection and creative thoughts on how to develop my business further. The benefit I get from this time is priceless. I can only recommend it to everybody."

3. Expressing Gratitude

*"A grateful mind is a great mind
which eventually attracts to itself great things."*

— Plato

This strategy is one of the most powerful ways to improve not only your mental health but every area of your life, thanks to the physical, psychological, emotional, and social benefits that come from living a life of gratitude.[1]

Dr. Paul Mills, a professor at the University of California San Diego, demonstrated that biomarkers of inflammation decreased by approximately 23 per cent over a two-month period in cardiac patients who maintained gratitude journals. Studying people who had depression, major anxiety, bipolar disorder, and schizophrenia, Mills found that gratitude and compassion supported their recovery because "it provides for us a sense of connection with not only ourselves but the world around us. And when we have more of a sense of connection, we feel more at home, we feel less stressed, we feel less depressed."[2]

In 2017, Professor of Psychological and Brain Sciences Joshua Brown proved that writing a gratitude letter every week for three weeks leads to significantly better mental health, irrespective of whether the letter was sent. Functional MRI scans revealed that those who wrote gratitude letters showed greater activation in the medial prefrontal cortex, a brain area associated with learning and decision-making, when they experienced gratitude, even three months after the letter writing began.[1] They

Writing a gratitude letter every week for three weeks leads to significantly better mental health.

1 - Bouchrika, Imed, "35 Scientific Benefits of Gratitude: Mental Health Research Findings," Reasearch.com, October 31, 2023, https://research.com/education/scientific-benefits-of-gratitude.
2 - Gutshtein, Natasha, "Research Shows Gratitude Practices Lower Inflammation," Gaia, March 8, 2022, https://www.gaia.com/article research-shows-gratitude-practices-lower-inflammation?gclid=EAIaIQobChMIy8uL3-L9-wIVV4BQBhOK8gW3EAAYASAAEgLrl_D_BwE.

also showed that people who are generally more grateful and gave more money to a good cause enjoyed greater neural sensitivity in the medial prefrontal cortex.

Here are the six recommendations from Harvard Medical School for cultivating gratitude on a regular basis:[2]

1. Write a gratitude note, letter or email, at least once a month, and write one to yourself every now and then.

2. Thank someone mentally.

3. Keep a gratitude journal and write in it every single day.

4. Count your blessings, taking time once a week to write what went well, including the good things in your life you hadn't even planned or hoped for.

5. Pray, if that is part of your practice.

6. Meditate by focusing on a positive word (like peace, calm, faith) or on what you're thankful for.

Constantin Bisanz's gratitude journey started in Peru, before he had his awakening moments. "I dislocated my shoulder while kitesurfing and I was in severe pain, when I was directed to an elder, a wise woman, who, besides helping me with my shoulder, gave me an energetic healing and offered the most precious advice, that changed my life: 'Start saying thank you for the little things - for a sip of pure water, for the ant that is crawling on your foot, for a bee or for a bird you hear in the distance. Not for the big things but for all the small details, and not only say it, but feel it. Train that gratitude muscle. And start talking to the universe, like the universe is your best friend, that knows all your secrets and from whom you can ask for any favour. Just do it for five minutes every day, but the more you can do it, the better. It will change your life - expect miracles! Beauty and miracles will unfold.'

"I thought, Well, that sounds simple. Sounds like something I've never done. I was curious and I started doing it. And everything changed - my whole life changed and keeps on changing, becoming more and more magical, like a red carpet is rolled out in front of me. I feel I have something I didn't have before. If you start nourishing yourself by appreciating the beauty that's already there, your life becomes magic. We're living already in heaven on earth, right? It's not in the future; it is already here. Only if we are able to recognise this, we can create magic in the future."

Reflection Questions:

• What are you grateful for?

• When is the best time for you to reflect and express gratitide?

1 - Brown, Joshua, Wong, Joel, "How Gratitude Changes You and Your Brain," *Greater Good Magazine*, June 6, 2017, https://greatergood.berkeley.edu/article/item/how_gratitude_changes_you_and_your_brain.
2 - "Giving Thanks Can Make You Happier," Harvard Health, August 14, 2021, https://www.health.harvard.edu/healthbeat/giving-thanks-can-make-you-happier.

"You don't have to be a monk in a monastery. You can have a mindfulness practice in every meeting, taking a minute to arrive, focus on your breath, get clear about what you want to achieve and how you want to behave. With a clear mind, you can understand reality, make better decisions, and drive a sustainable growth in your business."

— Michael Hengl

4. Mindfulness

"If you were conscious, that is to say totally present in the now,
all negativity would dissolve almost instantly.
It could not survive in your presence."

- Eckhart Tolle

From Sophocles, Goethe, and Blaise Pascal to Eckhardt Tolle, Deepak Chopra, Joe Dispenza, Jon Kabat-Zinn, and Daniel Goleman, philosophers, spiritual teachers, and scientists alike have stressed the importance of living in the present and paying attention to our thoughts, feelings, and sensations without any judgement or attachment. Today, we call this mindfulness.

As entrepreneurs, there will be, of course, times when you are going to need to plan ahead and reflect on the past in order to learn from your experiences. However, too much focus on the past and future robs you of the present moment. Eckhart Tolle sums it up nicely: "Most humans are never fully present in the now, because unconsciously they believe that the next moment must be more important than this one. But then you miss your whole life, which is never not now."

Michael Hengl stresses the importance of mindfulness in our personal and business life: "We all are used to eating twice or three times a day, which is a normal habit that gives your body energy. Most people also have a hygiene routine every day: take a shower, brush their teeth, and they feel comfortable afterwards: cleaner, healthier, and more relaxed.

Focusing on my breath is my shortcut to be right back in the core of myself, quiet and calm.

Not a lot of people have good mental hygiene, so the mind gets dusty storing one worry after the other, and the discomfort just grows and grows. What I do and recommend is a daily mindfulness meditation practice, to see what's there and try to understand what's real and what's just imagined. You don't have to be a monk in a monastery. You can have a mindfulness practice in every meeting, taking a minute to arrive, focus on your breath, get clear about what you want to achieve and how you want to behave. With a clear mind, you can understand reality, make better decisions, and drive a sustainable growth in your business."

Constantin Bisanz takes it even further: "I think 'mindfulness' is actually the wrong word. It should be 'mind-emptiness,' because only when the mind is empty are we able to learn and understand what life is really about."

Regula Curti, founder of Seeschau - House of Sacred Arts and of Beyond Foundation and Beyond Music, highlights the importance of breathing and breathwork as a pathway to mindfulness: "Mastering my breath allows me to become present, connected with my body and my inner world. We all know that when we're very nervous or stressed, we stop observing ourselves and start looking outside for the source of our discomfort. We end up frustrated, with unrealistic expectations about changing other people and situations we have no control over. We try to calm down the trouble outside when the trouble is inside. By mastering my breath, I master my body, my mind, and access my full potential. I have the ability to constantly observe myself and my thoughts. Focusing on my breath is my shortcut to be right back in the core of myself, quiet and calm."

Whether you regain your focus on the present moment through breathwork or by other means - making an effort to practice mindfulness will help keep your mind calm and alert, instead of frazzled with worry about past regrets or future fears.

CHAPTER SEVEN

5. Meditation

"Meditation takes you beyond the mind's noisy chatter into the pure awareness that is the source of all your happiness, inspiration, and love."

— Deepak Chopra

In a hectic world like ours, we assume we are high-functioning machines, able to operate twenty-four hours every day, without a break. We forget that even the best-performing engines are scheduled for regular checks and recalibration. That is why taking time every day to quiet our minds should be obligatory for us.

A mind in constant motion, relentlessly thinking and reflecting, is prone to negative thoughts. Nature programmed the conscious part of our brains to keep us safe from danger. Although we are rarely in life-threatening environments nowadays, our minds remain on constant watch. Thus, the goal of meditation is to quiet this continuous chatter and stop your thoughts from going left and right. Focusing on our breathing helps: by fully noticing each inhale and exhale, our minds are less likely to enter a negative spiral, without differentiating what is real or just imagination. In addition to breathwork, you may choose to listen to music, imagine relaxing scenery as you meditate, or repeat a calming phrase or mantra (such as "ohm," "peace," or another word or phrase that relaxes you). There are also apps available for meditation, such as Headspace, Calm, or Insight Timer.

Conny says, "When it comes to meditation, I have my own way. Again, it's not something I learned, but it's what made sense to me. During my hour or two of sports every day, I always include slow movements, exercising with my eyes closed. I might have some music in the background, helping me to relax and zone out. For many years, this has become my moving meditation - I move my body and clear my head. Some thoughts from the day will come, but step by step, I process and let them go, so by the end of my sports session, my mind has calmed down and I am not taking the stress of the day to bed with me."

He continues: "After the gym, I give my brain a moment of complete stillness and deep relaxation by going to the sauna. What is so special about this? First, I have no phone in the sauna with me. All the demands and stressors of the real world are parked outside. I visualise toxins and worries leaving my body through my pores and, after the cold shower or bath at the end, I dive into a moment of pure bliss. I lay down with my eyes closed and enter an almost out-of-body experience. A unique sense of floating, as I feel that euphoric state."

6. Developing Coping Skills

"You have power over your mind - not outside events.
Realize this, and you will find strength."

— Marcus Aurelius

Every person on earth has their own problems or challenges. The question is how we deal with them mentally. Life is 10 per cent what happens to us and 90 per cent how we react to it. When you go through a very difficult time, you need to activate a coping mechanism to stop your mind from going into a negative spiral.

One powerful tool you can use to calm down and be in the flow is music. Working on a playlist and finding the right music can be an easy way to relax. Another tool is to utilise a strong distraction. Conny recalls a time when he was stressed about a business partner. Every time he would think of the good times of their business venture or remember the disappointing moments, he knew he would become frustrated. So, to keep his thoughts under control, he decided that every time the partner's name came to mind, he would immediately think of football, which he loves (and it relaxes him). He says, "I know, it might sound silly, but trust me, this diversion saved me a lot of arguments and sleepless nights, not to mention conversations and actions I would regret later."

"The primary cause of unhappiness is never the situation,
but your thoughts about it."

— Eckhart Tolle

For many people, when their mind chatter is too loud, working in their garden or simply taking a walk or a run are good ways to work out any nervous energy through physical activity. Once they discharge that extra energy, they are ready to return to work, more focused and able to concentrate.

Our friend Mia Forbes Pirie, mediator, coach, and author, advocates for the importance of "continuously developing a clear, strong, kind, and discerning mind." She describes it as a mind that can stay present and calm and maintain self-esteem in the face of adversity, and if all else falls away, a mind that knows how to listen to intuition and follow it.

It's important to be consistent. It's not really about knowledge, as most of us already know what coping mechanism works best for us. In stressful situations, you must resist the overwhelming feelings and remember to access that specific tool, like going straight to your emergency first aid kit when you've cut yourself in the kitchen accidentally. You put a bandage on the injury to stop the bleeding; you don't leave it to fill the entire place with blood.

To be able to do that, you need to develop your self-awareness. Contrary to cutting a finger, we are not always aware of the mind's distortions. It takes a lot of training initially because we often don't even realise we are thinking negatively. It takes us maybe thirty seconds or more to realise, "Oh sh*t, I'm thinking again about this stupid thing." That is when you have the choice and the power to develop your mental muscles and become better at handling everything life throws at you.

7. Maintain Physical Fitness

*"Physical fitness is not only one of the most important keys
to a healthy body, it is the basis of dynamic
and creative intellectual activity."*

— John F. Kennedy

We stressed the value of physical activity for your overall health in the previous chapter, but it is important to address it again here, as it is so beneficial to mental health. We have all experienced at least one instance of that "feel good" sense following intense physical activity. Despite that, we sometimes forget to use exercise as a tool to re-balance our mood.

Recent studies demonstrate that the euphoric feeling - that "runner's high" - we experience after intense exercise results from the combined release of endorphins and endocannabinoids.[1] The additional dopamine released impacts our heart rate, sleep cycles, mood, attention, learning, and

Physical activity is proven to promote neuroplasticity, which is essential for our adaptability and learning.

motivation. The increase of oxygen supply to the brain due to physical exercise leads to increased executive function, expressed through working memory, flexible thinking, and self-control. Last but not least, physical activity is proven to promote neuroplasticity, which is essential for our adaptability and learning.

Exercise not only relieves stress but also acts as a self-confidence and mood booster. It can manage the symptoms of depression and anxiety, bipolar disorder, obsessive-compulsive disorders, and post-traumatic stress disorder, as demonstrated through a vast body of research.[2]

Whatever physical activity you choose is irrelevant: the important part is to choose something that works for you and that you notice a benefit from.

*"True enjoyment comes from activity of the mind
and exercise of the body; the two are ever united."*

— Wilhelm von Humboldt

1 - Linden, David J., "The Truth Behind 'Runner's High' and Other Mental Benefits of Running," John Hopkins Medicine, Accessed December 31, 2023, https://www.hopkinsmedicine.org/health/wellness-and-prevention/the-truth-behind-runners-high-and-other-mental-benefits-of-running.
2 - Preiato, Daniel, Collins, Ryan, "Exercise and the Brain: The Mental Health Benefits of Exercise," Healthline, May 10, 2023, https://www.healthline.com/health/depression/exercise.

8. Acts of Service

"The more I help out, the more successful I become.
But I measure success in what it has done for the people around me.
That is the real accolade."

— Adam Grant

Have you ever noticed that when you help a friend or donate to a charity, you feel happier? If so, this is no accident: ever since ancient times, philosophers have highlighted the connection between our well-being and our compassion and giving.

Science has been able to demonstrate how compassion, empathy, and giving, through the release of the hormone oxytocin, decrease anxiety and mitigate the effects of too much cortisol (from stressful situations). Several studies have shown that people who participate in volunteer work feel happier, appreciate the good in their lives more deeply, and live longer. People spending money on someone else experience increased levels of happiness, while spending money on themselves will not have the same impact.[1]

"It is when we give, that we feel most abundant," beautifully says Arianna Huffington in her book *Thrive: The Third Metric to Redefining Success and Creating a Happier Life.* In redefining success, she includes well-being, wisdom, wonder, and giving (in addition to money and power). It's true: making a habit of demonstrating small gestures of kindness impacts the world - as well as your mind and body.

1 - Allen, Summer, "The Science of Generosity," Greater Good Science Center, May 2018,
   https://ggsc.berkeley.edu/images/uploads/GGSC-JTF_White_Paper-Generosity-FINAL.pdf.
2 - DiGiulio, Sarah, "In Good Company: Why We Need Other People to Be Happy," NBC News, January 9, 2018,
   https://www.nbcnews.com/better/health/good-company-why-we-need-other-people-be-happy-ncna836106.
3 - Cunnington, Ross, "Neuroplasticity: How the Brain Changes with Learning," Science of Learning Portal, September 18, 2019,
   https://solportal.ibe-unesco.org/articles/neuroplasticity-how-the-brain-changes-with-learning/.

9. Connection with Others

"Deep human connection is ... the purpose and the result of a meaningful life - and it will inspire the most amazing acts of love, generosity, and humanity."

— Melinda Gates

We humans are a social species and, regardless of whether we are extroverts or introverts, we cannot live in isolation. The lockdowns we all experienced in 2020 reminded us that when contact with other people is restricted, levels of stress and anxiety can reach damaging levels. From Aristotle, who wrote, "Man is by nature a social animal," to the most recent studies demonstrating that "we are built to seek social companionship and understanding" (Emiliana Simon-Thomas, PhD), the unanimous view is that we need to live surrounded by other people to be mentally healthy.[2]

As entrepreneurs, we are always interacting with others. Those of us who are extroverts and natural-born networkers feel that we are recharging our batteries whenever we talk with others. There is, however, an interesting phenomenon that occurs when things go wrong: a tendency (even in the most extroverted person) to start avoiding people and carrying the burden alone. This is not only bad for business but also for your mental health. Those are the moments when you need to reach out for connection even more, share your problems with the people you trust, and ask for help. Never underestimate the therapeutic effect of deep, honest conversations and the power of two hearts and minds coming together.

We delved into cultivating positive relationships in a previous chapter, but in the meantime, consider these wise words from Albert Einstein: "A human being ... experiences himself, his thoughts and feelings, as something separated from the rest, a kind of optical delusion of his consciousness. This delusion is a kind of prison for us, restricting us to our personal desires and to affection for a few persons nearest to us. Our task must be to free ourselves from this prison by widening our circle of compassion to embrace all living creatures and the whole of nature in its beauty."

10. Keeping the Mind Sharp

"The greatest investment a young person can make is in their own education, in their own mind. Because money comes and goes. Relationships come and go. But what you learn once stays with you forever."

— Warren Buffett

When we say mentally active, we are not talking about spending hours on social media each day. We are talking about learning something new - either a language or a new skill - such as reading a book or listening to a podcast that broadens your perspective. Learning new things allows for the formation of new neuropathways in your brain, keeping it young and in the best possible shape.[3]

"Once you stop learning, you start dying."

— Albert Einstein

Mastering Your Mind for Strength, Resilience, and Focus

Personal growth is critical, no matter how you define success. You must commit to improving yourself over time to get the most out of life. While you can achieve a lot with dedication, discipline, and resilience on your own, you can turbocharge your personal growth with a coach and a mentor! John Wooden, one of the most successful American basketball coaches, rightly said: "A good coach can change a game. A great coach can change a life."

Through effective coaching, you are guided out of destructive, limiting beliefs which block you more than anything. It's the same when you get a great life coach or a business coach, depending on what you need the most. No one doubts the impact of a coach, as we

A great coach can change a life.

know that no athlete or team can become a world champion without that support. Yet, most people hesitate to work with a coach when it comes to improving confidence, achieving that scary personal dream, or exponentially growing your business.

Georg Graf von Walderdorff remarks, "Most people act from a subconscious mind programmed by past experiences, and that prevents them from growing. A coach can show you how to bring the subconscious into conscious, can help you understand it and work with it, in order to be able to walk a successful path in life."

"My strategies for developing a strong, clear and kind mind," shares Mia Forbes Pirie, "include maintaining the health of my body, mindfulness, meditation, breathwork and yoga. It is critical for me to know what my values are - as a result, knowing what success really means to me and following my purpose. Last but not least, I am humble enough to know that I have blind spots, so I work with others who can help me - coaches, mentors, therapists, etc. Never trust a coach who doesn't have a coach!"

J. Loren Norris, corporate trainer for leadership, attitude, and communications skills, gives the simplest yet most powerful advice to his clients: "If you cannot see where you are going, ask someone who has been there before." In business terms, this means getting a mentor.

Your growth journey will inevitably take you through times when you will feel extremely uncomfortable. In the last couple of years, all three of us have realised that as much as we hate it, real growth happens outside our comfort zone. Conny recalls: "Most of my life, I was very fortunate to feel in control, as I was the one giving directions to others. The world seemed to be turning around me. This is the reason why I did not develop more tolerance to discomfort. And this goes down to the smallest things, like having the patience to wait. It is even more difficult when people around you tell you all day how important you are. Only in the last one or two years has the word resilience become a companion for me."

Increase your tolerance for discomfort. Stay naturally grounded - even if the world turns around you. At some point or another, you will encounter discomfort in your life. Train yourself to respond gracefully to small daily challenges and do things you are not used to so discomfort becomes less threatening. Accept business opportunities which scare you, and don't give up when faced with adversity.

If there is only one thing you take away from this chapter, it is that **you can *train your mind!*** In the beginning, it might feel artificial, like telling yourself to think positively or making an effort to meditate, reflect, or stay in silence. As you start mastering these techniques, you will become a different human being - clarity and happiness will become part of your nature. We strongly believe that mastering your mind is a key ingredient to success. To build powerful habits for life, we recommend you start small and see how you can make it fun and easy to include in your normal routine - so you don't stop after a few days and say it doesn't work. Ask yourself how you can make it enjoyable to be consistent.

Reflection Question:

- Which of the ten practices will you begin including in your daily routines? Pick just one to start with.

LET'S REVIEW

In this chapter, you learned that your mental state is extremely important to your success as an entrepreneur and for living a full, engaging life. The collection of ten winning strategies will also help you develop a healthy mind.

Although burnout and mental health issues are commonplace today, they don't have to be! By incorporating the following practices into your life, you can combat burnout and ward off threats to your mental health: positivity, self-reflection, gratitude, mindfulness, meditation, coping skills, service, connection with others, and sharpening the mind.

WHAT'S NEXT

As we have seen, keeping your mind sharp and constantly improving your mental fitness results in numerous professional and personal benefits. It is also critical to understand the impact our emotions have, as together with our mind and body, they affect the quality of our lives. For this reason, the next chapter will delve more deeply into the importance of emotional well-being as a key component to your success as an entrepreneur.

CHAPTER EIGHT

Navigate the Depths of Your Emotions:
Understand "Energy-in-Motion"

"Genius is the ability to renew one's emotions in daily existence."

— Paul Cezanne

HARNESSING THE POWER OF EMOTIONAL AND SOCIAL INTELLIGENCE

In my opinion, emotional intelligence and social intelligence are the most underrated aspects of business success. We have focused too long on the typical "cognitive intelligence," or as some people call it, "Einstein" intelligence." However, when I look at many successful entrepreneurs, they do not excel in this conventional type of intelligence. Instead, they are exceptional at motivating their teams and captivating customers and investors - even without having a brilliant product - due to their emotional and social intelligence.

Yet, in our society, we are not "allowed" to display emotions. Children are often stopped by their parents when they have emotional outbursts: "Come on, you are a boy! You should not cry," or if they get overexcited: "Please calm down and behave yourself." In the end, we are all emotional beings. What matters most is how you make people feel. If I want to deliver a memorable, impactful speech for a special occasion like a marriage, funeral, or anniversary, I cannot numb myself. I put a lot of emotion into my speech. I can genuinely laugh and cry easily and have no fear of showing emotions.

In considering these realisations, I concluded that a key ingredient to success in life was my ability to express and create emotions in everything I did, from interactions with business partners to speaking on stage or celebrating achievements with my team. By this, I mean making people laugh, showing vulnerability, and carefully selecting the right setting for different purposes.

For example, for my last business dinner in Singapore, it was not only important to select the best restaurant for my guests, but also to include a walk in a park before dinner to create a more personal connection. As I spent time with five other people, I brought up more neutral topics, careful not to put people "on the spot" by discussing personal issues. I prefer to discuss personal things one on one, because in those situations, people open up more easily. With emotions, I always want to make an impact that people will remember years later. And they do.

For me, music is one of the greatest tools for transmitting emotions. Music can evoke and enhance emotions. Sometimes, we like to listen to romantic music because we are in love or our heart longs for something. Other times, we prefer joyful music because we love to dance. Each occasion calls for different types of music. Music can also help us connect with our emotions. We like listening to a song's melody as well as the song's lyrics, since any song is a short story - and many times, it relates to something we experienced in our own lives. The more a song's narrative fits our personal story, the more we enjoy the song.

Even though I am super optimistic, I sometimes like to listen to sad music. There is beauty in feeling the sadness, and it facilitates reflection. I can cope with my sad feelings the best when I listen to sad music. It is freeing to just allow yourself to feel whatever emotions come to your consciousness. And then, after I listen to sad music for some time, I switch over to something happy. This opens my mind, and I can approach my problems in a better way.

More or less, we all have the same problems: our hearts get broken, we make people suffer, or we worry about different things. Music is my way, my therapy, to access, process, and regulate my feelings. I have created my Spotify playlists to perfection, being able to evoke the atmosphere I need for all kinds of situations. If you are interested, you can find some of my best playlists on Spotify.

When you make a playlist and share it with friends or the one you love, it is a way to express your feelings and emotions. Music plays an important role in creating the perfect atmosphere, and for that reason, it's a constant presence in my life. I believe that, in order to have the right discussions and energy (and therefore the desired outcomes for different occasions), music helps create the perfect setting, in both business and personal life.

In addition to understanding my own emotions on a deep level, it is also important for me to empathise more with those around me. Even though I am an emotional person, I noticed that I expect people around me to be less emotional. I am not tolerant enough to accept their fluctuations; however, most of the time, I expect them to deal with mine. I know this is not fair, so that is something I continue to work on.

The challenge is that you can't selectively numb the emotions you don't want to feel. Most of us experience the negative emotions as intensely as we feel the positive ones. Or you might repress your emotions, but then you run the risk of becoming less emotional overall, not fully feeling positive as well as negative emotions, which starts to limit how you experience life and the choices you make.

- Conny

The Quest for Heart and Mind Harmony

"To feel these feelings at the right time, on the right occasion, towards the right people, for the right purpose and in the right manner, is to feel the best amount of them, which is the mean amount - and the best amount is of course the mark of virtue."

— Aristotle

Aristotle, one of the most progressive minds of his time, emphasised the importance of our emotions more than fourteen centuries ago. However, we needed the past twenty-five years of advancements in medicine, psychology, and sociology to understand the brain circuitry that is responsible for our emotions. This has allowed us to finally acknowledge the undisputable impact emotional intelligence has on the success of our lives, businesses, and personal relationships. We are lucky to live in a time when we not only know the importance of our emotions but also have access to the tools and techniques to master and respond effectively to people and situations around us.

For years, we have associated emotions with "matters of the heart" and outright dismissed them in business settings. We built societies and organisational cultures that worshipped our thinking minds and belittled any display or acknowledgement of emotions. In fact, in some societies, it is an unwritten rule not to show emotions. Still, our emotions are the universal language of our bodies' innate knowing. It's the way danger, desire, or despair is signalled to us, instinctively, before the evolved part of our brain can translate it into thoughts, words, or actions. Irrespective of your race, gender, age, geographic location, or culture, we will feel the same emotions (and recognise them in others).

Most of us haven't been taught to identify, distinguish, accept, and befriend our emotions. So, generation after generation, we ended up suppressing them - and we have become brilliant at distracting ourselves from unpleasant feelings with food, alcohol, TV, shopping, drugs, sex . . . and the list goes on! For many of us, the "ideal" state is one of numbness, in which we feel safe when we no longer feel any unpleasant emotion. While we may think repressing emotions is smart, it is actually 100 per cent damaging, because the result is that we make no real connection with what we truly want, need, or desire. We function on autopilot, buying what is advertised to us, believing what we're told, and (despite satisfying the urges we have) living with a deep sense of discontent. We do this because we're totally disconnected from our feelings; consequently, we no longer hear what our body is telling us we need.

"In the Western culture, we are overvaluing our mind, the intellect, and dismiss the heart contribution."

— Schoscho Rufener

Having worked with spiritual leaders over the past ten years, including His Holiness the Dalai Lama, serial entrepreneur Hans-Jürg "Schoscho" Rufener has learned that our minds are not the only currency of value in this world. "We have good emotional potential, but as we are so strongly trained intellectually, analysing, trying to be very precise, and integrating the world, there's this strong danger that we're not connected with our own emotions or with our feelings. This can be dangerous, as neuroscience has proven that the heart sends more information to the brain than the brain sends to the heart. So, we have much better connectivity with our heart than we think. The moment we learn to listen and find a way to access what our heart is saying in terms of our emotions or feelings, we have a broader perspective of how we can approach the world. This does not mean being against the intellect or having the mind against the heart. It is about how you combine them. It's like a band which sounds harmonious when integrating different sounds. We as human beings play our best when we access those two different contrasts - using both mind and heart intelligences."

> **The moment we learn to listen and find a way to access what our heart is saying in terms of our emotions or feelings, we have a broader perspective of how we can approach the world.**

Why Are Emotions Important in Business?

"Some of the greatest moments in human history have been fuelled by emotional intelligence."

— Adam Grant

When Conny reflects on his life as a founder, investor, and business angel, he confirms that being in the right emotional state and having the right attitude has been instrumental in leading negotiations and winning business pitches. Emotions are the energy connecting people, so his mantra is: "If you fundraise without emotions, don't even start."

The same applies to inspiring your team: don't bother sharing your vision for the future, or motivating them through challenging times, if you've not energised yourself and are not in a positive emotional state on that day. Our "why" - which is our passion, translated into the emotions and energy we broadcast - is the only direct and authentic way to connect with clients, business partners, and investors to receive that yes from them at the end of the conversation.

Schoscho Rufener reminds us of the power of creating emotions and what strong leverage that is, not only

in the entertainment and events business, but also every time you want to reach out to people and captivate your audience - whether you are a speaker, an artist on stage, or a host at your home.

We have the same basic emotions we had a million years ago. At that time, our fear protected us from losing our lives, like when being chased by a lion or a threatening neighbour. While we still experience fear, we must now be aware that, even if we feel fear in front of a board of challenging bankers and it seems like our entire life is at stake in that negotiation, our life is not being threatened. We need to develop coping mechanisms so that fear does not take over, causing us to self-sabotage. When too many worries accumulate, anxiety is no longer a protective mechanism. "Modern" stress can erode our health until we break down. The sooner we're aware of emotions being out of proportion to an actual event, the more easily we can restore our confidence and calm.

While most of the events we experience daily are not as threatening as our nervous system perceives them, ignoring and suppressing your emotions can be life-threatening, as shown by a 2013 study done by Harvard School of Public Health and the University of Rochester, which found that people who "bottle up" their emotions increase their risk of a premature death from any cause by more than 30 per cent, and concomitant risk of being diagnosed with cancer by 70 per cent.[1] Suppressing your emotions affects not only your health but also your creativity. Over time, if you're not connected with your emotions, you will start making decisions with your brain only, and you will soon lose that "gut" feeling - those instincts that are crucial in aligning you with your bigger truth.

In *Emotional Intelligence: Why It Can Matter More Than IQ,* Daniel Goleman dismantles our belief in IQ supremacy

If you fundraise without emotions, don't even start.

and offers a clear understanding of the importance of emotions and the active role we can play in enhancing our EQ, with a direct positive impact on our lives. He identifies five components of emotional intelligence described in the book: self-awareness, self-regulation, motivation, empathy (social awareness), and relationship management (social skills).

---

1 - Chapman, Benjamin P., Fiscella, Kevin, Kawachi, Ichiro, Duberstein, Paul R., and Muennig, Peter, "Emotion Suppression and Mortality Risk over a 12-Year Follow-Up," Journal of Psychosomatic Research 75 (4) (2013): 381–85.

Mastering Your Emotions

To help you master your emotions, we like Daniel Goleman's approach by explaining, exemplifying, and providing tools for the five essential components so that you can build a strong foundation, one brick after another.

1. Self-awareness

"Knowing others is intelligence, knowing yourself is true wisdom; mastering others is strength, mastering yourself is true power."

— Lao Tzu

Although we use the terms "emotions" and "feelings" synonymously when describing what we're going through, there is a difference between the two of them. Emotions are "real-time data, sparked by sensations in our body," explains Rachel Allyn, PhD. They are like raw data, originating in the subcortical region of our brain, the amygdala, and the ventromedial prefrontal cortex, causing biochemical reactions to occur and change our physical state.[1] The best example is to think of the flight or fight reaction you had when confronted with a dangerous or stressful situation. Do you remember sensing a certain level of anxiety, manifested by your heart beating faster or your palms sweating? In this instance, you are experiencing primal emotions, which are unconscious and instinctive.

According to psychologists Paul Ekman and Wallace Friesen, there are six basic emotions that all humans can experience: happiness, sadness, fear, disgust, anger, and surprise. Studies confirmed there are universal facial expressions, often accompanied by sounds, which are associated with them. This is universal human signalling we all share. You will never mistake a grimace made by someone disliking their food, irrespective of the country they come from.[2]

Our feelings, on the other hand, are conscious experiences, influenced by our emotions and generated from our thoughts.[3]

Knowing that most of our emotions are triggered, and therefore we are not always in complete control of them, Schoscho Rufener believes in the power of self-awareness and intentionality when it comes to what we feel. "Most of the time we are not masters of our emotions, but the more we progress on our growth journey, we can be more responsible for our emotions. There is a huge potential in realigning oneself, learning which trigger leads to an emotion and being aware how you feel in each moment. I believe that it is our responsibility to be clear about the quality of emotions we want

---

1 - https://www.psychologytoday.com/gb/blog/the-pleasure-is-all-yours/202202/the-important-difference-between-emotions-and-feelings
2 - https://www.betterhelp.com/advice/general/feelings-vs-emotions-is-there-a-difference-between-them/?utm_source=AdWords&utm_medium=Search_PPC_c&utm_term=PerformanceMax&utm_content=&network=x&placement=&target=&matchtype=&utm_campaign=1692973502&ad_type=responsive_pmax&adposition=&gclid=CjOKCQjwqoibBhDUARIsAH2OpWim8FmeqnbYZBS3-m-a3SJhFKY2t0u8LY7WGAXMvSSAhwZQLOLYhX0aAnxJEALw_wcB
3 - https://counseling.online.wfu.edu/blog/difference-feelings-emotions/

"Emotions are
what make us human.
Make us real.
The word 'emotion' stands
for energy in motion.
Be truthful about
your emotions, and use
your mind and emotions
in your favour,
not against yourself."

— Robert T. Kiyosaki

to live in. Your life quality will enhance as you are start to master, or just accept the work of those emotions which are important for you, and for your future."

When we stop and listen to our body, we become aware of the emotion and can ask ourselves if it is a correct reflection of reality or if we are just being triggered because of a painful experience from our past and we're overreacting.

For many people, even labelling the emotion or the feeling will be something totally new. But the more you practice, the better you will become at recognising it.

In her last book, *Atlas of the Heart,* Brené Brown clarifies the importance of labelling emotions:

Trusted people are not the ones who will only tell you what you want to hear. They need to be people you respect for their competencies, honesty, and values.

"Language is our portal to making meaning, connection, healing, learning, and self-awareness. Having access to the right words can open up entire universes. When we don't have the language to talk about what we're experiencing, our ability to make sense of what's happening and share it with others is severely limited. Without accurate language, we struggle to get the help we need, we don't always regulate and manage our emotions and experiences in a way that allows us to move through them productively, and our self-awareness is diminished. Language shows us that naming an experience doesn't give the experience more power, it gives us the power of understanding and meaning." Important research shows that we can actually shape feelings by naming them. *Not* having access to emotional language decreases our ability to interpret emotional information from others.

Labelling emotions is transformative, according to Harvard psychologist Susan David. She goes on to note that people who manage to distinguish between a wider range of emotions can navigate the ebb and flow of everyday life and not overreact to the typical challenges most people face on a daily basis. When considering an entrepreneur's life, isn't that life simply a series of ups and downs we need to manage?

To improve in naming your emotions, you don't need to enrol in a psychology course; Brené's book mentioned above is a fabulous resource. You can also start using an emotion wheel - a circular graphic representation of a wider range of emotions, derived from the primary ones - to increase your capacity to differentiate what you're feeling.[1]

Katja Hengl Bellingshausen, tech investor and chairwoman of 1492 Holding, believes that "Self-awareness is absolutely key for having a successful business and being a good leader. Because if you don't know yourself, you become a risk for yourself, for the people around you, and for your company."

---

1 - https://humansystems.co/emotionwheels/

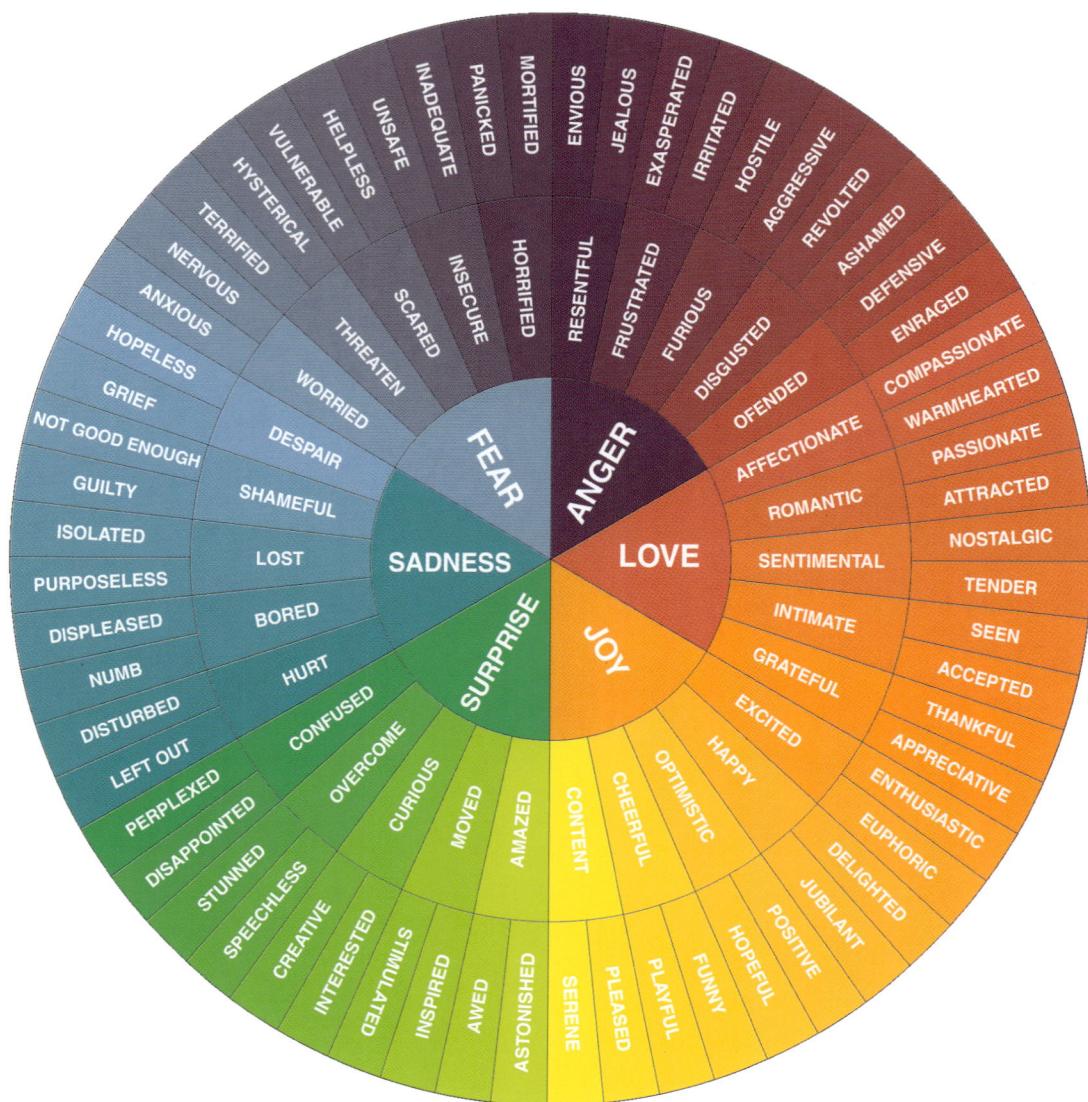

Other important steps in increasing your self-awareness are saving time for introspection and asking for feedback from trusted people. Katja sees feedback as "an amazing gift from others that allows us to learn and grow as humans and leaders. A healthy feedback culture is essential in any organisation." The distinction we want to make here is that trusted people are not the ones who will only tell you what you want to hear. They need to be people you respect for their competencies, honesty, and values. That is the feedback you can rely on.

Reflection Question:

- Who can provide you with honest, relevant feedback, so you can become more self-aware?

"The gold standard that will revolutionise your life," says Mia Forbes Pirie, an expert in using somatic transformational models, "is being able to physically feel and fully accept the sensations in the body, giving rise to the feeling as well as to name the feeling. When that is possible, an increased sense of stability, presence, calm, and clarity arises. Particularly if they can be held in awareness with the right attitude, the right level of warmth, calm, lightness, and kindness."

2. Self-Regulation

"Between stimulus and response, there is a space.
In that space is our power to choose our response.
In our response lies our growth and our freedom."

— Victor Frankl

In his book *Emotional Intelligence: For a Better Life, Success at Work, and Happier Relationships,* Brandon Goleman explains that, while we may be tempted to follow certain pleasurable impulses, self-regulation will help us remain true to our long-term goals - and this will keep us focused on long-term, sustained contentment and happiness.

Emotional self-regulation is important to avoid saying or doing things we will regret. Think back to a moment when your emotions got the better of you. Despite any awareness of your strong emotional state - and knowing you might ruin that holiday or jeopardise that deal - you still blew off steam and caused damage. If you've ever had anything like this happen, have the courage now to ask yourself if expressing your emotions in that way was worth it. Most likely, the answer is no.

When we interviewed Katja, she shared a brilliant practical approach for self-regulation: "When you're triggered, and my goodness we all are getting triggered by different situations, the first step I can recommend is just do nothing! Even when you want to scream or cry. Just try to do nothing and let it sit. Take a deep breath and then reflect on the situation. Is this a pattern repeating over and over again? Where does this pattern come from? Take another breath and then react. Just give yourself the time and not react to any single trigger coming from the outside."

Schoscho Rufener shared the importance of having a good thermostat to measure how you feel in the moment, so if you don't feel well, then you can adjust your mood: "Most of the time I'm very aware of how I feel and how I interact and react to other people within a second; if I'm strong or weak or sensitive or inspiring. I always try to reset myself – take tiny little steps, adjusting, to be in charge of my feelings, of how I interact, that I don't get triggered. If it's too intense or too dark, then I try to take time off: I love to sit in front of a fireplace, go for a walk, do some bodywork, or sit by the water to re-energise myself, on my own. Sometimes it might take time, but I try to define the intensity of the moment and approach the topic slowly. Because if you open all the doors to intense emotions, it's too hard to handle. If you have some intense situation in life, it's good to have a professional, a coach, or a hypnotherapist where you can have your protected space and this gifted person can help

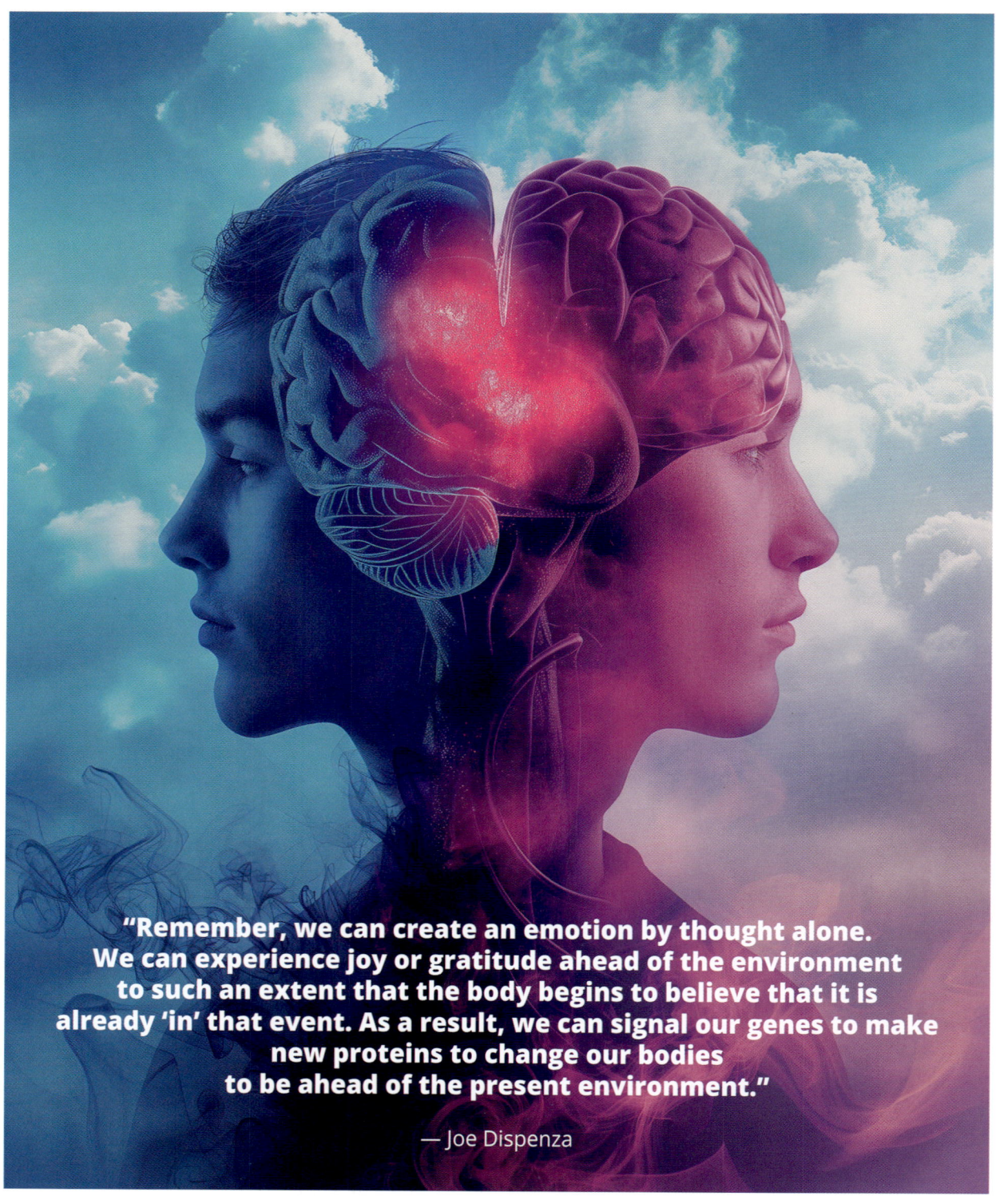

"Remember, we can create an emotion by thought alone. We can experience joy or gratitude ahead of the environment to such an extent that the body begins to believe that it is already 'in' that event. As a result, we can signal our genes to make new proteins to change our bodies to be ahead of the present environment."

— Joe Dispenza

you approach the emotions, or provide a different angle, to find a way of accepting, or dealing with the topic."

Brandon Goleman is correct in saying, "You will not always be able to control how you feel about something, but you can control how you handle those feelings." For this, he recommends three important steps:

Define your personal values because that is what keeps us grounded. Our values will be the North Star, guiding us to the decisions beneficial to us. They might change throughout life, but knowing where you want to stand will make your emotional responses so much easier to control.

You will not always be able to control how you feel about something, but you can control how you handle those feelings.

Commit to take personal responsibility for your actions. You may be saying, "I am a responsible person!" Well, our invitation here is to stop for a minute and think of one thing that didn't go according to your plan. Notice who or what you blamed – and then try to find the 3 per cent you might still be responsible for.

The truth is, we cannot control what someone else does, but we can always lessen the drama and not repeat our mistakes. A basic example is the escalating frustration you feel when you are stuck in the morning traffic, arrive late, and feel stressed during your first morning meeting. As a result, you may put extra pressure on your team, instead of being calm and curious. Of course, you cannot change the morning traffic, but when you take radical responsibility for your life, you admit that having left home half an hour earlier would have led to a different outcome. Or, while you were stuck in that traffic, as you noticed the build-up of negative emotions that were taking control of your morning, you could have chosen to use the time for some mindfulness exercises to keep yourself calm and better prepared for that meeting.

Decide to establish "calm and collected" as your main mood. Once you decided you want to be calm, you can start practicing that state so you have more access to it when you need it. And incorporate changes in your life that will make you calmer, like reducing your caffeine intake, getting more sleep, or processing your emotions by journaling, exercising, and meditating.

This ties into Mia Forbes Pirie's view that your attitude is key. She asks, "Can you do your best to make your attitude towards whatever arises, calm, kind, and curious? Can you maintain that attitude even towards the emotions that are not at all calm, even if you can't control those emotions directly?"

"Attitude is king," says Mia. She believes that "We often misplace our efforts if we focus simply on trying to change our feelings. The key to inhabiting better states is to change our attitude towards both our feelings and the events that are unfolding. We have limited direct control over our feelings as they arise, but we have far more control over our attitudes. Feelings come and go, often uninvited. Our attitudes can change both our feelings and the level of energy and resourcefulness we have, to respond to events. So, if we choose to have a calm, warm, friendly, lighter attitude towards feelings and events, we get different outcomes."

3. Motivation

Motivation is the catalyst for our most courageous actions and the fuel behind our resilience when faced with difficult times in our lives. Motivation is connected to our emotional quotient (EQ) because it gives us the power to do the things that make us happy, making us more adaptable and charismatic at the same time. Who would like to spend lots of time surrounded by people who are disengaged, complaining, and have no clue or desire to achieve something in their lives? If you are reading this book, we bet you are not such a person. Your motivation radiates like a lighthouse, in the dark of the night, be it good or stormy weather. It's contagious and self-charging.

Now, we would like to push you outside your comfort zone, so your motivation becomes even more powerful. For the next twenty-one days, perform this exercise when you wake up in the morning: imagine that the vision you have for your life is already happening now. What are you feeling? What are you seeing, hearing, smelling, or touching? As you anchor yourself in the vision which motivates you the most, ask yourself, "What is the one thing I can do today to get closer to that moment?" Even the smallest step you take will make a difference and keep that dream alive.

4. Empathy

Besides managing emotions through self-regulation and motivation, it is critical to develop your empathy, so you can read the emotions of the people around you. Become aware of the energy in the room. That will tell you a lot before anyone starts to speak. Learning to observe what other people might be feeling requires a practice, but the rewards are worth the effort.

Empathy is the pre-requisite to recognising emotions in others, so we can adapt our approach – words, tone of voice, attitude, and actions – to better connect or influence the person we are interacting with. Empathy is our ability to be aware and understand someone else's emotions ("walking in their shoes") and to experience life through their perspective. Doing this only takes willpower and practice.

You can start with cognitive empathy: look at life from someone else's perspective and stop yourself before throwing the usual judgments you might have. The next step is experimenting with emotional empathy. You do this by opening your heart to feel what the other person is feeling. If this is new for you, have confidence that you can do it. If you ever felt the energy and adrenaline surge during an action movie, or the sadness and heartache when your favourite team lost a game, then yes, you can empathise. The mastery level is compassionate empathy, where you not only acknowledge and feel someone's suffering, but you *take action* to alleviate that. This is something many of you are already doing when you invest your time, energy, or money in helping friends in times of trouble or supporting charities that speak to your heart.

**Your motivation radiates
like a lighthouse, in the dark of the night,
be it good or stormy weather.
It's contagious and self-charging.**

CHAPTER EIGHT

5. Relationships management

After being able to understand yourself, manage your own emotions, and resonate with the emotions others have, you're finally ready to relate with the people around you. Social skills refer to your ability to communicate appropriately, persuade and inspire your team, and manage conflict effectively. Conny says, "Mastering my emotional state is key for my business success as connector and investor. When operating in my best emotional state, I have the confidence to become the most charismatic, inspiring, and persuasive person in the room. "

Conflict is one of the areas that you might need to work on most - because it is not a question of if but when you will experience conflict in your life. Hoping the problem will disappear or avoiding it will not work, since you will still experience the repercussions of repressed emotions. If you want to thrive in a healthy emotional space, then conflict management is a skill you must learn!

As Mia Forbes Pirie states in her book on how to move away from polarisation towards connection: "The real test of any emotional skills we develop is, of course, in relationship with others. For most people, it's relatively easy to stay calm on your own and conflict is the 'peak challenge' situation that tests all our emotional intelligence. Conflict can take us right back into that fight, flight, or freeze mode and disempower us. Some people end up more aggressive and not able to fully listen and take in information from the person they're in conflict with. Others become more passive and not able to stand up for their own interests. Both have negative consequences because you need to be able to both listen and to speak up for your interests and needs. It is much more difficult when you are personally involved than as a mediator or coach. The key is to be aware of your emotions and your intentions and not be overly attached to how the other person reacts." Staying calm and using the strategies in this chapter can help you handle conflict.

Mia also advises that it is important to remember, when you listen, that understanding someone and agreeing with them are not the same – and talking over people rarely works as a strategy for achieving the best solution (even though we may sometimes think it does!).

When you are experiencing conflict or overwhelmed by emotions, don't be afraid to ask a friend, no matter how much you think you need to figure it out alone. Sometimes, a professional can help you have conversations that you otherwise would avoid for many years. In certain situations, a mediator, with additional confidentiality, can also help everyone find solutions they never thought of before and keep everyone calm, slowing the conversation down for people to hear each other, communicate, and listen the right way.

Creating a Vision for Your Emotional Life

Schoscho Rufener's ideal of a good life is one lived at high vibrational energy. He strongly believes that life is about energy - sharing, giving, and receiving energy. "Strive to be mature enough to really find the best in any interaction - to make the best of what I need while understanding what the other party is looking for. So, if there is no resonance, be clear and step out in a nice way. The more you practice, the more freedom you get and the less a**holes you meet on your journey. Or if they pop up, you're much clearer how to handle those situations."

Schoscho highlights that when you are yourself, clear and clean from an emotional and energetic perspective, this helps other people to feel safe and open up. His goal is to always have a "lightness, an easiness of life," so when he approaches a topic or whatever challenge comes his way, he is well prepared: "I imagine having a black belt and being ready to face the next challenge, which results from feeling good in my body, being well-trained, and then combining it with my intuition and heart."

"The only way we can change our lives is to change our energy
– to change the electromagnetic field we are constantly broadcasting.
In other words, to change our state of being,
we have to change how we think and how we feel."

— Joe Dispenza

Reflection Questions:

- What is your vision for your emotional life?

- What will you gain if you develop your emotional intelligence?

- What is the first action you can take to better navigate your emotions?

Our friend Constantin Bisanz brilliantly summarises the transformational aspect of emotional connection: "All emotions are energy that wants to be acknowledged and move on. E-motion = energy in motion. Just being able to fully connect with a person on all levels of transparency and honesty and with a 100 per cent% open heart without any limitations, has brought a completely different quality to my life."

"The energy that actually shapes the world springs from emotions."

— George Orwell

Conflict resolution
is a skill you must learn,
because it is not
a question of
if but when you will
experience conflict
in your life.

LET'S REVIEW

Emotions matter – and they are extremely important to get in touch with as an entrepreneur! By working on your self-awareness, self-regulation, motivation, empathy, and social skills, you will find that your business and personal relationships will improve, and your ventures are more likely to succeed. As you raise your emotional quotient, keep your personal life vision in mind. This will motivate you and serve as your North Star when you are tempted to give up, repress your emotions, or allow strong emotions to overwhelm you.

Realising how much energy and information emotions hold can make a huge difference in your life. The more you get in touch with your emotions, the more power you can generate by directing that energy towards achieving your goals. Don't be afraid of showing your emotions, and learn to give people space to express theirs. Repressing emotions leads to negative consequences everywhere – from your private and business relationships to wider society. We need a safe space to express how we feel and to be heard. Exploring the depths of our emotions and learning from them enhances our emotional intelligence, empowering us to navigate challenges, build resilience, and cultivate richer connections with ourselves and others.

WHAT'S NEXT

Once you have raised your emotional quotient, you are ready to "level up" and improve your spiritual life. Although many people may consider their spiritual life to be something separate from their personal, nothing can be further from the truth! As you tap into the power of a fully evolved spiritual life, you will find that this can become an infinite source of energy, resilience, creativity, and joy.

CHAPTER NINE

Spiritual Journey:
The New Key to Success?

"When you examine the lives of the most influential people who have ever walked among us, you discover one thread that winds through them all. They have been aligned first with their spiritual nature and only then with their physical selves."

— Albert Einstein

MATERIAL . . . OR SPIRITUAL?

Whenever I meet interesting, fascinating people, I notice that they all have something in common: there is something they live for that is higher than themselves. I have also observed that when people have this higher purpose and vision, they become more successful. That led me to wonder if this happens unintentionally, or if living life in this way is something you can learn.

I used to ask my dad, "Why are you going to church every Sunday?" He answered that he believed in something bigger than himself and that going to church helped him reflect on the different topics the priest was bringing up every week. Many people who don't believe in God still believe in something greater than themselves. Ever since I was a child, I believed that one person's god was no better than another's god. In my opinion, all religions communicate the same message, and they also share the same purpose: to love others, live with compassion, and have faith that their higher power is doing what is best for their greatest good. Many times, their religious beliefs support them in times of suffering. As a result, this phenomenon - believing there is something or someone "up there" - helps mankind feel a sense of protection and security. Sadly, churches have taken advantage of people's faith and abused their position of power and control.

Spirituality is not something new, but what is new is the "packaging" and messaging. Today, spirituality has become a version of religion that works for many people. And as more individuals find their faith in a way that is not tied to any dogmatic religion, churches are becoming emptier, while spiritual events like Burning Man are booming.

As an entrepreneur, if your only meaning in life is work, you will find yourself unfulfilled at some point in time. Embracing your spiritual side helps to enhance your work life and fills you with a sense of meaning, purpose, and faith in something greater than yourself. For many of us, spirituality is an inner compass for our beliefs and values; when you feel you are in alignment with your core values, you find the energy to go the extra mile.

I like the practical approach to spirituality: meditation, mindfulness, and self-reflection. Interestingly, when you consider different religions, many of them employ these methods in some way.

About ten years ago, I began opening my mind and became interested in spirituality. It was the first time I read about it, and I found myself admiring people whose lives have a purpose larger than themselves. They were conscious - and I realised I was not. I was never present; instead, my thoughts were always someplace else.

I know that when some people hear the word "spirituality," they may react negatively. While I do not ask anyone to agree to a particular set of beliefs, I do ask that you open your mind and drop the stereotypes you may associate with spirituality. When you release judgment, you just might find (like I did!) that your life becomes immeasurably better.

One thing we can probably agree on is this: spirituality means different things to different people. But this is a topic most people do not discuss when chatting with a stranger - or even friends. For some, it is not even a conversation they want to have with themselves. So, you may be wondering, why discuss spirituality with others, even if it's friends or family, when we can keep the conversations simple and light? Isn't it easier to ask about work, school, or the most recent holiday? And why do entrepreneurs need to think about being spiritual?

Think back to your teenage years. There is a good chance you pondered the big existential questions: What is the purpose of life? Why am I here? Is there any existence after death? Maybe at some point you even debated those topics with friends, late at night after a party . . . or maybe you were curious enough to discuss the subject with parents or teachers. It is also likely that, in response to your questions, you would have been told to stop wasting time and just focus on passing those exams and on getting that first well-paying job so that you could start a family. Only to realise, many years later, that material possessions and achievements did not answer your burning questions – and none of your successes quieted your desire to explore the spiritual side of life.

- Conny

"The foundations of a person are not in matter but in spirit."

— Ralph Waldo Emerson

WHAT IS SPIRITUALITY?

"That is the real spiritual awakening, when something emerges from within you that is deeper than who you thought you were. So, the person is still there, but one could almost say that something more powerful shines through the person."

-– Eckhart Tolle

Many people confuse spirituality with religion, and although they have commonalities, someone can be "spiritual" without belonging to a specific church, synagogue, mosque, etc. Equally true is the fact that many people consider themselves religious but are far from spiritual.

Religion is a specific set of organised beliefs and practices, usually shared by a community or a group. It implies the belief in, obedience to, and reverence for a superhuman power or powers. Over time, religions have led to well-defined socio-cultural systems and, besides promoting good values, often generate division in the world.

Spirituality, on the other hand, is having a strong sense of higher purpose and meaning - bigger than your daily striving for survival or success. It is unique knowing that there is a field of energy you are part of that influences, connects, and unites everyone. Another part of spirituality is the inexplicable belief in a higher power or intelligence that communicates with us in unexpected moments in the most surprising ways.

"It is through gratitude for the present moment that the spiritual dimension of life opens up."

— Eckhart Tolle

Have you ever felt in awe of a breathtaking landscape? Maybe you're on a ski holiday, and after a foggy morning, the sun's rays suddenly break through the clouds. In that split second, an entire valley you couldn't see before now appears in front of you, twinkling like thousands of sparkling diamonds. Or maybe you're sitting at your computer, and the moment you glance out the window, you realise the sky has transformed into a spectacular sea of fire. Or maybe you have experienced moments when your heart is totally flooded with the deepest possible feelings of love because your newborn baby smiled at you, or your lover touched your hand. In these instances, when you feel immortal, invincible, and deeply vulnerable at the same time, you may think, "I wish I could freeze this beautiful moment in time forever!"

For a few seconds, time stops, and you reach a level of bliss you never imagined possible. It is in those moments that your inner knowing tells you that there is more to life than "this world." And you experience deep gratitude for having had a glimpse of infinity. That *is* an example of spirituality.

In spiritual moments, some individuals instantly realise that there must be a divine hand behind all that is. Some people actually feel the spark of divinity inside, resulting in an unquestionable level of faith, peace, and acceptance of whatever will come next in their lives.

We love Brené Brown's interpretation: "Spirituality is recognizing and celebrating that we are all inextricably connected to each other by a power greater than all of us and that our connection to that power and to one another is grounded in love and compassion. Practicing spirituality brings a sense of perspective, meaning, and purpose to our lives."

No wonder the New Age movement replaced the word God with Love. Consider the words of Marianne Williamson, who helps us understand the essence and importance of love: "Love is what we were born with. Fear is what we have learned here. The spiritual journey is the relinquishment - or unlearning - of fear, and the acceptance of love back into our hearts. Love is the essential existential fact. It is our ultimate reality and our purpose on earth. To be consciously aware of it, to experience love in ourselves and others, it's the meaning of life."

Williamson rightly considers that, when we attach meaning to things that aren't love (like the money, the car, the house, the role we have), we can be lost in a dark, parallel universe. This world becomes a place where we love things more than people. We begin placing more value on what we perceive with our senses than what we know to be true in our hearts. Instead of focusing on this material world, we need to express our love in those intangible - but much more profound - ways. How do we do this? Demonstrating selflessness, generosity, and care toward those around us is how we express authentic love.

David Wetton, founder of Spirit in Work, Ltd., shared that one of the vows he took when he became an Interfaith Minister is to love, honour, and nurture the Divine in all those I meet. This way of living allows him to remain true to himself, regardless of what is happening around him. For him, spirituality is finding meaning and purpose in all aspects of your life (relationships, work, etc.). Through David's lens, the moment we are interested in the meaning of our lives, we have begun to connect with our spiritual dimension.

Sometimes, our spiritual journey can begin with the willingness to explore something new, like observing a tree for a week - a method David uses with his clients. "Just by sharing or reflecting on what you have discovered and by being curious, we start noticing incredible things, not only about the natural world but also about us and how we are all interconnected. This journey of reflecting on ourselves, expanding our emotional intelligence and our spiritual intelligence, is not about getting the answer. It's more about opening up to a way of being and doing in life, which is so nurturing."

Michael Hengl passionately shares his view on the importance of spirituality: "We need to remember that our spiritual life is the foundation; it's not a by-product or a side dish. In the absence of your moral and spiritual dimension, life is not sustainable. If we only focus on finite games, it's not enough. It is very risky to become a professional idiot, dealing with your subject matter expertise, who - in the absence of a broader perspective - ends up harming left and right his family, co-workers, business, or environment. And that cannot be part of the future."

Michael also suggests that as you grow into your spiritual self, you discover freedom - a freedom

"When we attach meaning to things that aren't love ..., we can be lost in a dark, parallel universe."

— Marianne Williamson

you could not experience when you only identify with your family, the village, your thoughts, or your body. Instead, you will understand that your identity transcends the material world, and as the rat race of constant competition and striving becomes less important to you, your fear drops . . . and you can live life without worry.

Science and Spirituality

Over the last century, Western society started worshipping science, the materialistic nature of our world, and the desire to have absolute power over the planet, the forces of nature, and other fellow humans. We gained knowledge and independence, just to wake up completely disconnected from each other, from the life surrounding us, and from our souls. We denied the role of spirituality. And like any form of fanaticism, our world's extremist views have resulted in the current climate crisis, universal feelings of profound isolation, and the highest levels of stress, anxiety, and depression our society has ever experienced.

In the early 1990s, shortly after he received the Nobel Peace Prize, the Dalai Lama participated in a five-day dialogue with a group of Western psychologists, neuroscientists, and philosophers. During these talks, he concluded that the purpose of spirituality in a secular world is that of a moral compass that tempers the destructive emotions of greed, hatred, and delusion that so often accompany our modern materialism. His Holiness said, "With the ever-growing impact of science on our lives, religion and spirituality

Science is not only compatible with spirituality; it is a profound source of spirituality.

have a greater role to play in reminding us of our humanity. What we must do is balance scientific and material progress with the sense of responsibility that comes . . . [with] inner development. That is why I believe this dialogue between religion and science is important, for from it may come developments that can be of great benefit to mankind."[1]

Carl Sagan, in his last book published in 1966, *The Demon-Haunted World: Science as a Candle in the Dark,* agrees with the Dalai Lama. As he explores the relationship between science and spirituality, he says that if we view science and spirituality as "mutually exclusive, . . .[we do] a disservice to both."[2] "Science is not only compatible with spirituality; it is a profound source of spirituality."

The good news is that, due to the tremendous progress made in recent years, neuroscience has proved that cultivating spirituality leads to greater grit, greater optimism, greater resilience, and conversely protects us against destructive tendencies. As demonstrated by Dr Lisa Miller, PhD, professor of psychology and education at Teachers College, Columbia University, research also supports that developing a personal spiritual practice can enhance joy and personal fulfilment, while ulti-

1 - Popova, Maria, "The Dalai Lama on Science and Spirituality," The Marginalian, Acessed January 27, 2024, https://www.themarginalian.org/2018/10/16/dalai-lama-science-spirituality-destructive-emotions/.
2 - Popova, Maria, "Carl Sagan on Science and Spirituality," The Marginalian, Acessed January 27, 2024, https://www.themarginalian.org/2013/06/12/carl-sagan-on-science-and-spirituality/.
3 - Miller, Lisa, *The Awakened Brain: The New Science of Spirituality and Our Quest for an Inspired Life*, Random House, August 17, 2021.

CHAPTER NINE

mately contributing to greater levels of well-being.[3]

With a landmark study in 2012, Miller offers scientific proof that we are all innately spiritual beings, born with a spiritual core - and when we become more connected with our spiritual selves, we are 80 per cent less likely to be addicted, 60 per cent less likely to take our lives, and we can be whole and thrive. Using MRI scans, the study showed that the high-spiritual brain was thicker and stronger in exactly the same regions that weaken and wither in depressed brains.[1]

The cortical thickening in the back of the brain near the parietal region - which is observed in people with high levels of sustained spirituality over time - is not only protective against depressive episodes and levels of depression symptoms, but also emanates high-amplitude alpha wavelengths (alpha is 8-12 Hz), similar to the brainwaves observed in the posterior brains of meditating monks and, notably, is "jump-started" in people using SSRI medications to treat depression. The results showed "in a physiological, material way that spirituality is a consciousness for which all of our brains are wired; and that, long-term, the spiritually engaged brain is a healthier brain."[2]

Using a functional magnetic resonance imaging (fMRI) technique in the attempt to map human thoughts, feelings, and experiences to specific regions of the brain, Dr Miller was able to define two levels of awareness we all have: "achieving awareness" and "awakened awareness."[3] To operate at our best, it is essential for us to integrate both types of awareness in our lives. She goes on to say,

> **"Achieving awareness is necessary. It helps us move and chase the ball up and down the field. But to decide where the ball needs to go, to see the bigger field of play, to be aware of the other players, to understand the consequences and impact of our choices - and to perceive why we are playing the game in the first place - we need our awakened awareness. In other words, our most important decisions can't be made from achieving awareness alone. We can only perceive reality accurately when we have both foundational modes of awareness on board."**
>
> — Lisa Miller

1 - Miller, *The Awakened Brain*, pgs. 51-52; 62-62.
2 - Miller, *The Awakened Brain*, pgs. 153-154.
3 - Miller, *The Awakened Brain*, pgs. 163-166.

"We are all magical, divine beings, equipped with a superpower that we cannot grasp when we're not conscious. We all have the divine intelligence in us, but we need to discover it."

— Constantin Bisanz

When Spirituality and Entrepreneurship Nourish Each Other

Our conversation with serial entrepreneur Constantin Bisanz had been an eye-opening moment about how entrepreneurship and spirituality can blend to create an extraordinary life. His journey of transformation was an inspiration for us, and we hope it will captivate and uplift you as well.

"I was an entrepreneur, but I had no idea about spirituality, even though I was practising transcendental meditation for twenty minutes daily for many years. I had this mindfulness practise, but I never believed in anything: nothing resonated with me. And then, a personal experience - the end of a seven-year relationship - led me to ask myself, 'Have you ever thought about your life?' And I realised that I have never really thought about it. I was just running like this, from the age of fourteen, when I started my first company, doing crazy things like extreme sports, starting seven companies, one after the other - and sometimes even starting a company only two hours after I sold the previous one. I was living a very, very hectic life ... but never reflecting on what was happening. I was *in* the system rather than being able to think *about* the system."

His true awakening unfolded during a trip to the Amazon rainforest, where he had the chance to meet the ancient Shipibo tribe. He learned about plant medicine and tried Ayahuasca, an ancient psychoactive "brew" used by indigenous people for spiritual and healing purposes.

From this experience, Constantin shares, "Layer after layer opened, blockages in my mind were removed, and I was able to see further. It was during my second ceremony when I received a clear message that there is so much more to life than what I thought. I believed I was *living the life* being a successful entrepreneur - but then I realised no, this was just a preparation for the immensely beautiful and magical life that was revealing itself to me. Everything we do - the success, the struggles, the failures, and getting up again - it's just like training a muscle ... and that I have been prepared to devote all my skills, abilities, and network towards supporting the divine creation. And so is everybody."
After his time in the Amazon, Constantin began seeing the interconnectedness of this world everywhere: from bacteria and fungi to plants and animals, he noticed that everything benefits the ecosystem. "Even though we don't like some bugs, they're essential for the biological equilibrium. So, I realised that we humans are medicine for other humans. We are all equipped with certain skills, and we have a Dharma, a purpose. We are all magical, divine beings, equipped with a superpower that we cannot grasp when we're not conscious. We all have the divine intelligence in us, but we need to discover it. Once we are on the path to discover this intelligence and our superpowers, we are helping the divine creation and evolution to truly explode and fertilise."

Constantin explains further: "Plant medicine work gave me a direction; I realised there's so much wisdom available, being able to connect with this higher intelligence. Based on that experience, I sold everything I had. I released myself from the hamster wheel, put all my responsibilities aside, and made myself available for my inner work. What followed were two years of 'spiritual ninja training': learning about myself, doing silent meditations, fasting, yoga, Qigong, Chinese medicine, and more plant medicine."
"I realised that it is possible to go very deep and inward quite easily, but this is not the real thing.

We can live a spiritual life being a monk in a cave, completely shutting off the daily challenges of a 'normal life.' What is not easy is to bridge the two worlds: spirituality and fulfilling your Dharma. As entrepreneurs, we are creators, and we not only have ideas, but we also have the skills to manifest those ideas into reality, right? So, how can we bridge this? This is the biggest challenge. Before, I was just an entrepreneur – running and creating, without this mind emptiness and spirituality, without knowing why I do this. Now that I had the chance to sit for two years in a cave, completely sheltered and learning about spirituality, my real challenge is how to embody this in everyday life.

"This is what we need to learn as entrepreneurs: to live a so-called spiritual, mind-empty life, with awareness, knowing our Dharma. Understanding why we do all this, why we want to be successful. Is it just for us, or does it serve the greater good of all? This is really what I realised: everything I used to do was very much centred on my ego. I wanted to be famous, be on the cover of a magazine, and have millions in my bank account. I wanted to have a beautiful house here, and a boat there, and blah, blah, blah. It was all about me, but not so much about what my contribution is. In other words, what is my gift to the world? Every tree has a gift. The tree provides shadow and oxygen, cleans carbonated air, and when it dies, it gives nutrients back and fertilises the soil. Some trees give fruit, too. This is what nature does, what every animal does. Then what is our gift? This is what I call spirituality: how can we put everything we do, as entrepreneurs, under the umbrella of a higher purpose, serving the greatest good of all, and how can we keep our intentions pure?

This is what I call spirituality: how can we put everything we do, as entrepreneurs, under the umbrella of a higher purpose, serving the greatest good of all, and how can we keep our intentions pure?

"Living a spiritual life is very similar to maintaining a garden. You must make sure you're planting the right seeds. So, what kind of seeds do I want to plant? Do I like carrots, do I like potatoes, do I like kale? What are the things I want to harvest? I need to think about the result I'm envisioning. Before we plant the seeds, I need to prepare fertilised soil. Most of the soil is not fertile, so I need to clean the weeds, take out the rocks, enrich the soil, and create the right 'bed' for my garden. Then we need to maintain it and nourish it, to help Mother Nature: take care there's enough water, enough sun, and continuously work on maintaining this garden, nourished and free of weeds and parasites, which are coming all the time.

"What I realised that really makes a difference, is to give love to this garden. We need to talk to the seeds and the plants, maintain them, and constantly give them love and care. So, this is what we should also do with our business: treat it like a vegetable garden for our family and not spray it with chemical pesticides. Do it naturally, helping it flourish."

When asked what a spiritual life means to her, Regula Curti, founder of Seeschau - House of Sacred Arts and of Beyond Foundation and Beyond Music, explains that "living a spiritual life is about leadership and mastering yourself." She believes that to be an awakened individual, you must cultivate a daily practice to do so. "The world as we know it is changing a lot, and all this is affecting us. It affects our minds. We must constantly digest what we hear, what we sense, and try to empty ourselves to go back to the clarity and the essence of ourselves, in order to have the strength to deal with what happens outside. You can be a leader outside only if you are a leader inside. So, spirituality is about my own leadership. It's about mastering myself, mastering my body, my nutrition, my thinking, and mastering my reaction to the outside world. Constantly clearing my mind and spirit to sharpen my visions, my motivation, my beliefs, my practices, becoming a master of it."

You can be a leader outside only if you are a leader inside.

Reflection Questions:

- What is your personal definition of spirituality?

- What would you like your spiritual life to look like in the future?

- As you develop your spiritual self, what impact would you like to make on your loved ones, your business, and the world?

Spirituality in Practice

Like everything in life, spirituality cannot be "achieved" by simply going on a retreat for two weeks and becoming inspired to reach higher levels of consciousness - and then returning home and doing nothing. If you follow that formula, you'll find yourself back at square one. Spirituality must be something you do every day. You need to develop your own practice, one that works for you: something you are motivated and energised to do consistently. Taking time to cultivate a spiritual practice - be that prayer, meditation, or just sitting in silence and being present - is essential for our congruence. Living in the present is the gateway to a spiritual life. Sadly, far too many people spend so much time anticipating the future that they lose sight of the present moment.

"If you want to terrify yourself, go to the future. And if you want to feel sorry, or sad, or have resentments, go to the past. Because today you are smarter than yesterday, so the judgments are obsolete and the regrets useless. Only in the present moment, everything resolves."

— Michael Hengl

Think about it: when you spend your day distracted by your past, you're wasting precious hours ruminating on, remembering, or regretting moments in time that have already passed. You cannot change those events - but you can change your behaviours, reactions, and thoughts *in the present . . . right now.* Sadly, if you live your days as a series of "if-onlys" or "what-ifs," you will never experience the magic of the present moment. So, instead of dwelling on things you cannot change, consider the positive difference you could make with your business and relationships if you simply choose to be mindful of each moment as it comes, interacting and behaving in a way that aligns with your core values and beliefs.

The same is true for the future: if you feel dissatisfied, anxious, or impatient about the future, and if you spend your time focused on events that have not yet transpired, you are (once again) missing the beauty in the present. Rather than distracting yourself with the future that has not yet happened, realise that what you do - or don't do - can positively impact that future you desire. And the more you remain grounded in the "right here and now," the greater the chance that your future will unfold exactly as you intended!

Michael's commitment to living in the present moment and not compromising on his daily spiritual practices starts by simply not grabbing his iPhone the moment he wakes up and focusing on his breath instead. You, too, can release the mind chatter and remain as focused on the present mo-ment as possible by counting each breath, working to improve the number of breaths in a row you can take before any intrusive thoughts enter your mind. This is an excellent way to build attention and focus, and you will find that the ability to remain present will begin to carry over to other parts of your day as well. You can incorporate this same practice at bedtime, too, leading to a more restful night of sleep.

> **Every time you connect with your highest self and act as a better version of yourself, you positively impact all areas of your life.**

Regula's spiritual life comes first, every morning and late at night, before she goes to sleep. In every moment, she tries to be as present as possible throughout the day, in her actions. One strategy she works on is mastering her breath, because breath is key in whatever we do. "My breath is everywhere with me, even in challenging situations, like when I am speaking at a business conference. Breath brings me back into my body, to remain present and connected. Mastering my breath helps me to become more conscious and even move toward higher levels of consciousness."

She also stresses the importance of discipline. To her, this means remaining disciplined with diet, exercise, and fulfilling commitments. "When we overindulge in a well-pampered way of life, we end up not moving enough, eating too much, sleeping less, or partying too long and even missing life-changing meetings we're not aware of. This is something many people don't like to hear. For me, discipline is not something I'm afraid of. Because I know that a disciplined life is an opening to everything I want to achieve."

David Wetton's practice is based on "cultivating a sense of knowing." One of the most frequent questions he gets from leaders is: "How do I know I'm living in alignment with what my soul wants?" He responds that part of the sense of knowing comes from observing synchronicities - and he knows that he is on track as everything starts flowing, from people to events and resources. "I have the sense that things in my life are made *through* me, and not by me."

Try this: call to mind those times when you ignored your "gut instinct," only to regret that decision later on. Moving forward, commit to honouring that sense of "knowing" - and acting on it - and you will find that your decisions come from a more peaceful place. Even if things don't work out as planned, you will be more likely to maintain a sense of perspective, knowing that everything is happening for a reason, and that usually (in hindsight), things tend to work out for your highest good . . . even it doesn't appear that way in the moment.

Here's one more exercise: the next time something good happens to you, think back to the synchronicities that took place to result in the perfect outcome. Ask yourself if there were any moments that you felt or "knew" everything would work out. The more you do this, the more you will realise that there are no coincidences in life! It is our hope that, with time, you will begin to sense that there is a higher power, supporting you, flowing through you - and that you are part of something bigger than you, in which you beautifully resonate.

Reflection Questions:

- What do you feel are the most important takeaways from this chapter?
- What spiritual practice(s) would you like to incorporate in your life?
- What steps can you take today to begin those practices?

Spirituality doesn't need to involve religious ceremonies and qualifying assessments. What is more important is your commitment to a larger good and that you connect deeply with the beings, events, and objects that surround you. It doesn't require mystical experiences but rather an open heart to the uniqueness and beauty of the world. Every time you remember that you can connect with your highest self and act as a better version of yourself, you will positively impact all areas of your life.

"We as entrepreneurs have a duty to think, how can this benefit the planet? How can this benefit humanity? How can this benefit nature and the creation because it's our duty? I think if we recognise that we will be supported by the divine forces, we'll have access to superpowers."

— Constantin Bisanz

LET'S REVIEW

Spirituality can be challenging to define, but at its core lies a desire to connect with something larger than yourself. When you open your mind to the possibility of the existence of forces more powerful than what we experience with our senses in this 3D world, life becomes magical. The drive for material things fades as you find greater fulfilment in connection with others, making a difference in the world, and leaving a legacy. To build your spiritual foundation, we suggest harnessing the power of presence, as well as getting clear on how your spiritual dimension will connect with the vision you have for your life.

WHAT'S NEXT

Once you connect with your spiritual side consistently, you will begin to experience happiness: the topic of the last chapter of this book. But take heed: this is not the fleeting happiness you feel with a new possession or accomplishment. Rather, we are talking about a type of happiness that is akin to pure joy, everlasting and deep.

CHAPTER TEN

Pursuing Happiness:
The Ultimate Goal?!

"I believe that the very purpose of life is to be happy"

— Dalai Lama

FAKE IT . . . UNTIL YOU MAKE IT

There's a legacy in our German culture that we should refrain from being overly optimistic and instead of encouraging a positive mindset, always examine the risk factors. This way of thinking is extremely negative and common to many Europeans who view everything as a threat and the glass as always half-empty. In fact, it is still common for children who express excitement and joy to be told by adults "Don't be so optimistic!" or "Be careful!" in an attempt to tone them down. In my opinion, these beliefs and behaviours hamper our ability to pursue true happiness.

Everybody experiences their share of positive and negative events, but I believe that happiness is an attitude. It is not so much what happens to you; it is more about your perception and beliefs surrounding those events, as well as your reactions to them. I recently had a discussion about happiness with my oldest son, Tassilo, after noticing that he was using a lot of negative language. When asking him to be more positive, he challenged me on this point, saying that too much positivity feels artificial, like sugar-coating. And I can understand how he feels this way, growing up in a society and educational system that praises moderation. Upon deeper reflection, I wondered if I should be more balanced; maybe sometimes, my positivity was too much. In the end, we agreed that he would work to speak more positively, while I would consider if my positive thinking was truly authentic and not leaning towards "toxic positivity."

I did not always consider myself a happy person, but that began to shift from the age of twelve. With parents who were always positive and in a good mood, I must have inherited good genes, making it easier to feel happy.

Currently, I am at a tipping point in life, reflecting on what made me happy in the past versus what brings me happiness in the present. I realised that something like the SPAC project - despite the sense of accomplishment and wonderful experiences - did not result in the lasting happiness I was hoping for.

One of my core beliefs is you don't have to be the richest in the graveyard. I can't take anything with me when I pass away. Just accumulating more of the things that made me happy in the past is no longer making me happy now. At the same time, a constant state of happiness is not realistic. For example, sometimes in life, you must complete tasks that are not fun, and you don't have much of a choice in the matter. That is just how life is, and instead of complaining - which is what I used to do! - it's much easier to simply complete the project without complaining. On these occasions, grumbling and whining will not help me reach a higher level of happiness. But if I just do it without complaining, the process is less miserable. And when the dreaded task is over, it is easier to regain a sense of happiness quickly.

At other times in life, you may be in a situation that appears negative at the onset but eventually becomes positive in the long run. For instance, let's say you separate from your partner; this can be a devastating event, if you are afraid that you will never find happiness again. But with time, you may be happier than you ever imagined, either on your own or meeting someone who is a better match for you!

One of the best pieces of advice I can give regarding happiness is to "fake it until you make it." This does not

You don't have to be the richest in the graveyard!

mean being insincere but rather, training yourself to remain optimistic, even in challenging circumstances. You will find that the more you react positively to people and situations, the more frequently you experience moments of happiness. Eventually, happiness will feel natural to you, and even during difficult times, you will bounce back much more quickly and easily.

Finally, it is important to remember that, when it comes to achieving happiness, there is always a period of time between setting a goal and achieving it. Nothing happens overnight; however, when you adopt the attitude that you will aim to be as positive as possible, no matter where you are on your journey, you will find these times of transition to be much more pleasant . . . even happy!

But the biggest shift happened when I turned fifty and came across the concept that our lives follow a U-shaped curve of happiness. Developed by economists David Blanchflower and Andrew Oswald in the early 2000s, after analysing data from various countries, the finding is that people's happiness tends to decline in early adulthood, reach its lowest point in middle age, and then increase again in later life, forming a U-shaped curve when plotted over time. The thesis holds that we begin out lives without worry, without awareness of the troubles of the world and (hopefully) with the support of parents or other guardians. As we enter the working world, we are confronted with the complexities of daily life, worries about achievement, success, financial security, and finding a life partner. We reach peak unhappiness in our forties and fifties, our mid-life crises, before happiness then begins its ascent again and we enjoy the freedoms of retirement. Visualising my entire life on one page woke me up to the value of every single day. Working on the optimistic assumption that I will live until the age of ninety, being fifty-five now, I have only about 12.784 days, 420 months or thirty-five summers ahead of me. I firmly believe that I am the architect of my own happiness, so I decided to make the most of every day I am left with. As you can extend your lifespan (living longer) and your healthspan (having a high quality of life as you age), I am committed to expanding my happiness-span too.

To the people accusing me of being addicted to happiness, I pose this question: if you could choose an addiction, wouldn't this be a good one? Instead of being a victim of your circumstances or other peoples' actions, seeing everything in dark colours and identifying yourself with your problems, isn't choosing happiness a better alternative?

— Conny

> **"Happiness cannot be travelled to, owned, earned, worn or consumed. Happiness is the spiritual experience of living every minute with love, grace, and gratitude."**
>
> — Denis Waitley

NAVIGATING THE PATH TO TRUE HAPPINESS

"We humans are so tortured by not properly guessing what will make us happy."

— Atticus

What better final touch on your ONE journey than to integrate everything we have explored so far toward living a happy life every day? The happiest people don't necessarily have the best of everything, they just make the best out of everything. They have the ability to perceive and appreciate the beauty in life's simplest moments.

We know from scientific research that money won't make us happier, yet so many people live from day to day focused on material things because they believe this is what will make them happy. In fact, a recent study on more than 1,000 students graduating from the University of British Columbia suggests that prioritising money over time may actually undermine our happiness.[1]

Unfortunately, many people do not reflect enough about what makes them happy. As a result, they may find themselves pursuing goals or activities that society or others deem important rather than those that truly resonate with their own values and desires. Engaging in regular self-reflection can help you identify and prioritize the sources of genuine happiness in your life

In the pursuit of understanding the science behind true happiness, Harvard conducted one of the longest longitudinal studies ever carried out on this subject. Robert Waldinger, director of the study, reached a conclusion that says it all: "The clearest message that we get from this 75-year study is this: good relationships keep us happier and healthier. Period."[2] In addition, "It's not just the number of friends you have, and it's not whether or not you're in a committed relationship,"[3] says Waldinger. "It's the quality of your close relationships that matters." The biggest predictor of your happiness and fulfilment overall in life is, basically, love. According to George Vaillant, the Harvard psychiatrist who directed the study from 1972 to 2004, there are two foundational elements to this: "One is love. The other is finding a way of coping with life that does not push love away."

---

1 - Whillans, Ashley, Macchia, Lucía, Dunn, Elizabeth, "Valuing Time over Money Predicts Happiness After a Major Life Transition: A Preregistered Longitudinal Study of Graduating Students," Science Advances, September 18, 2019, https://www.ncbi.nlm.nih.gov/pmc/articles/PMC6750911/#R2.
2 - Harvard Medical School, "Welcome to the Harvard Study of Adult Development," Accessed January 30, 2024, https://www.adultdevelopmentstudy.org
3 - Harvard Medical School, "Welcome to the Harvard Study of Adult Development."

CHAPTER TEN

General Considerations for Happiness

Happiness is highly subjective and different for each individual. What makes you happy might not be the same for someone else. For this reason, happiness is extremely personal.

Happiness also implies a learning process - your journey to find out what really makes you happy. When you start out in life, you might chase what you've seen other people enjoy or like, from a need to fit in with a certain group at a particular time. Therefore, it takes some trial and error to discover what makes you happy. The process is similar to trying out different hobbies. Some people like to play football, while for others, playing a sport might seem like the worst idea ever. They may prefer walking or reading instead. Considering these personal preferences and variances, you need to give yourself time to find out what makes your heart sing.

Things will change over time, too, so what made you happy as a teenager might not make you happy as a young adult or later in life. As you grow, evolve, and discover different aspects of life, you will develop different needs and interests.

"The best path to happiness is learning to change as rapidly as life does."

— Miguel Angel Ruiz

There is a distinction between short-term and long-term happiness - or short-term pleasure and long-term fulfilment, to be more specific. There are two ways of looking at this. One is being willing to sacrifice immediate gratification - that instant boost of happiness - for the bigger game we play in life. The other is intentionally giving yourself small bursts of joy, even during the toughest times. You don't need to forge ahead with frustration, anger, and pain towards your ambitious goals. Instead, stop for a few minutes and be grateful for your steps forward and the lessons learned. Allow happiness to enter your life from simple moments like looking at the blue sky, smelling your coffee, or just being alive.

The list of synonyms for happiness is impressive: bliss, contentment, delight, exhilaration, pleasure, and euphoria are just a few. As we dive into this conversation, you might be developing a better sense of the kind of sustained happiness we are discussing. In this chapter, we aim to explore the deep, profound sense of happiness we can experience, in all its complexity. Even though we can start by looking to the outside for what makes us happy, in the end, happiness is an inside job and a choice we must make repeatedly, until it becomes our reality.

In her TED-X talk, "Happiness Is a Choice," Katja Hengl Bellingshausen, chairwoman of 1492 Holding and tech investor, makes a great point: "We so often override reality with the cruel stories our mind creates. Our mind is trained to focus on what is not working."

When we interviewed Katja, she explained further: "You can always choose between going into a fear-based reality and going into a joy-based reality. There are always two sides, and it's up to us to choose which way we're going. You can train your mind

Happiness is an inside job, a decision we must consistently reaffirm until it becomes our reality.

to get out of the suffering by discovering your fear-based thoughts, even if you're not aware of them in your normal consciousness. Then you intentionally replace all these stressful thoughts in your head with positive ones."

Happiness: Nature or Nurture?

There are moments in life when happiness is the last thing on our minds, like when we lose someone dear to us or encounter challenging medical or family problems. During crises, you would question your sanity if you were not suffering or sad. However, feeling constantly unhappy is not good for your mental health and quality of life.

It is interesting how, after spikes in happiness, if something in your life changes for the better, you will quickly return to your "typical" level of happiness. This is validated by a theory in psychology known as the hedonic treadmill (or hedonic adaptation), which states that people repeatedly return to their baseline level of happiness, regardless of what happens to them.[1]

You might argue that happiness levels are uncontrollable, and you cannot escape from the patterns you currently experience. Fortunately, this is not the case – and there are measures you can take to increase your happiness quotient!

Sonja Lyubomirsky, in her book *The How of Happiness*, offers research-based evidence to demonstrate that 50 per cent of our happiness is the result of genetics, 40 per cent comes from how we see life and adjust to it, and only 10 per cent is the result of external factors.[2] Isn't it inspiring to realise just how much impact we can have on our own happiness internally, and how insignificant external events, which are beyond our control, truly are?

Capitalising on that 40 per cent you can control is worth it, when you consider the results of a meta-analysis of 225 studies on happiness, presented at the 2016 "Happiness & Its Causes" Conference in Sydney. At this conference, Professor Lyubomirsky showed that happy people are more productive at work and more creative, make more money, have better jobs, and are better leaders and negotiators. Happy people are more likely to marry, have fulfilling marriages, and are less likely to divorce; they have more friends and social support, have a stronger immune system, are physically healthier, and live longer lives. They are more helpful and philanthropic, and they also show more resilience to stress and trauma.[3]

1 - Schaffner, Anna Katharina, "How to Escape the Hedonic Treadmill and Be Happier," PositivePsychology.com, September 5, 2016, https://positivepsychology.com/hedonic-treadmill/
2 - Lyubomirsky, Sonja, The How of Happiness, Penguin Books, December 30, 2008, Pg. 20.
3 - Happiness & Its Causes, "The How of Happiness with Sonja Lyubomirsky, PhD, at Happiness and Its Causes 2016," YouTube, March 23, 2018, https://www.youtube.com/watch?v=F7JDbP_x8So

The Fundamentals of Happiness

Achieving happiness is intricately tied to several key practices we have presented in the previous chapters of this book. Still, to have everything in one place, we are mentioning them here too. Firstly, **expressing gratitude** and appreciation for what we have fosters a mindset of abundance and contentment. **Learning to forgive** allows us to let go of resentment and negative emotions, freeing ourselves from emotional burdens. Practising acts of kindness not only benefits others but also brings a sense of fulfilment and connection to our lives. **Investing in relationships** nurtures a support system that enhances our well-being and provides a sense of belonging. Furthermore, **committing to meaningful life goals** gives us direction and purpose, guiding our actions towards personal fulfilment. **Regular meditation** and a **spiritual practice** offer moments of introspection and peace, aiding in emotional balance and inner harmony. Lastly, **engaging in physical activity and exercise** not only improves our physical health but also boosts our mood and energy levels, contributing to overall happiness and well-being.

It takes a lot of inner work to have happiness as our default state: letting go of the beliefs that don't serve us, to return to the essence of love and happiness we are all born with.

We believe it all starts with **monitoring how you talk to yourself.** Self-compassion will not come easy if you always focus on criticising your mistakes. This will only make you miserable! The key to living a happy life is to accept yourself exactly as you are. You might not be perfect, but no one is! We do not advocate accepting behaviours that don't serve you. Rather, commit to your growth and take strong actions in that positive direction, while accepting the things you cannot change.

Always build on your strengths! The beauty of being an entrepreneur is that you can create your life around your unique qualities, instead of trying to fit in a place that doesn't value what you bring. If you want to take it to the next level, simply praise yourself every day: "I'm amazed at how good I am at this!"

The beauty of being an entrepreneur is that you can create your life around your unique qualities.

The second fundamental of happiness is to **stop comparing yourself with other people.** In the age of social media, we end up with a distorted impression of reality. We don't see the true story behind those pictures on the beach, with the luxury car or with the perfectly dressed, well-behaved children. If only we knew what someone's life looked like, behind the camera lens, we would never even consider swapping our lives with theirs.

We also need to **stop idealising the past or ruminating on things we cannot change.** We have this incredible ability to view things that have happened in the past in a much more positive light than how they really were. At other times, we can't stop thinking of previous events, and we beat ourselves up with regret, guilt, and shame. Both approaches keep us stuck in a continuous state of regret, and it's deeply unhealthy.

Living in the past - even with a "positive" bias - is just as harmful as making your happiness conditional on an ideal future. If you continuously believe that you will be happy when you get your degree, or when you make your first million, or when you find that perfect partner, you prevent yourself from enjoying the present. What's even worse is that once you've achieved that goal, your happiness will be short-lived.

The alternative to living in the past or future . . . is to **start living in the present!** The more conscious you become, the more you observe when your thoughts are somewhere else. To combat your mind's tendency to wander to the past or future, remember how good you feel when focusing on one thing only, living in the power of the present. Learning to be more conscious in the moment means making an effort to put the phone down and really listen during a conversation to understand the other person better. Or focusing on the flavour and textures of your food during lunch, instead of eating in front of your computer, thinking at your next presentation.

Decide the fundamentals of happiness you need to add to your life and become religious about incorporating those practices into everyday living. The pursuit of happiness takes work, but it is so worth it.

Reflection Questions:

- What is one area of your life in which you can stop comparing yourself to others?
- How can you engage in more positive self-talk? How can you be more present?

"**Happiness is when what you think, what you say, and what you do are in harmony.**"

— Mahatma Gandhi

The House of Happiness

Achieving happiness is like building a house: you set a strong foundation using the fundamentals we mentioned in this chapter, and then you continue by adding the "rooms and floors" tailored to your specific needs during various life phases.

You must build your own house of happiness over time. It's not given to you in a nice box with a silk ribbon the day you are born. Even with a solid structure, you still need to continue building it every day. Whatever areas you decide to work on, enjoy expanding this edifice that will provide you strength and a sense of security.

We believe you need security in many aspects of your life to feel happy, because - unless you are a Buddhist monk, at peace with every moment of your existence - it is quite difficult to feel happy if you cannot pay your rent, are at risk of losing your business, or your life partner just left you for someone else. The more aspects of your life in which you feel secure, seen, known, accepted, and loved, the better.

But what happens when parts of your life are out of balance or uncertain? Or what if you simply fear the unknown? Sometimes, it helps to think about the worst-case scenario - and then acknowledge that whatever happens, even if you lose everything, you still have yourself and your skills to start again. This simple act of reassuring yourself, even under the worst circumstances, can help remove feelings of fear and helplessness.

Reflection Questions:

- What are your essential needs to be happy?

- What is under your control?

- What is one adjustment you can make to build a more stable house of happiness?

Happiness: It's a Choice

"Research has shown that the best way to be happy is to make each day happy."

— Deepak Chopra

Realise that you always have choices. Even when you fail, you can succeed again in life! And when it comes to fear and anxiety, remember this: if we look back at our lives, we will realise that 70 - 80 per cent of the concerns or worries we had never even happened. And, when they did happen, most of the time, the result was not as bad as we initially thought.

One of the best pieces of advice on the uselessness of worrying we've seen was the one Gaur Gopal Das gave us during a presentation at the 2018 Unternehmenrtag. This is his genius algorithm, which requires no explanation:

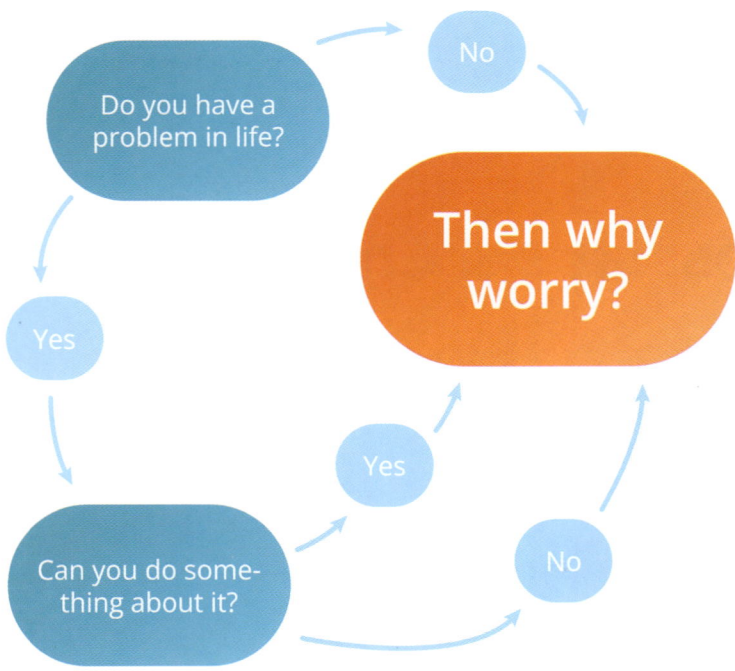

Happiness is a process, not a result - and if you get something too easily, the reward does not mean as much. Regardless of what you're experiencing right now, the simple act of waking up in the morning is a gift we receive every day. It is a reason to start each day with a smile on your face.

We have shared ideas to boost your level of happiness. However, everyone is different, so we invite you to choose ways that make you happy, even when some things are not going exactly the way you want.

A big, big part of our happiness comes from our work, because we spend at least half (if not two-thirds) of our waking hours at work. It makes us sad when we hear that most people who go to work are not happy with what they do. If work is half of your life, then a big part of your happiness must come from it: being unhappy with what you're doing for any length of time will affect your overall happiness significantly. It is essential to find a job that not only gives you pleasure but also long-term happiness if you want to live a fulfilled life.

"Happiness and business belong together," Katja Hengl Bellingshausen asserts. "If you don't like it and you're not happy with what you do, you are at high risk of burnout because you live in a constant state of stress. And when you love your work, you will be able to accept all business situations, setbacks, and failures as necessary components to building a successful business, so the state of happiness you're in energises you to move forward."

To strengthen your resilience, try widening your perspective. Consider our Planet Earth, a mere speck of dust orbiting an average-sized star, the Sun, which is just one of billions in our galaxy, the Milky Way. Zooming out further, our galaxy is but one among more than two hundred billion galaxies in the known universe. And yet, even the enormity of the observable universe, with its hundreds of billions of galaxies, is just a tiny fraction of the potentially infinite multiverse. In this perspective, the scale of human existence fades to near-nothingness against the backdrop of the cosmos. Our concerns, ambitions, and struggles appear minuscule and fleeting in comparison to the grandeur and vastness of the universe, reminding us of our humble place in the cosmic tapestry.

What Makes You Happy?

"Happiness develops when you are working on something bigger than yourself. It is attained slowly, little by little, as you build yourself up. It develops as you develop your altruism. You find happiness by committing to other people and positivity, by working to better yourself and find real meaning in your life."

— Robert Gill Jr.

For Henry Cookson, founder and CEO of Cookson Adventures, ultimate happiness is to spend time in raw nature, with people you care about or you've newly met, and see their appreciation of what it is. Aware that this is not a place where he can stay the whole time, Henry counts on his insatiable curiosity and passion for preserving Planet Earth to continue his quest for happiness. "What makes the deepest satisfaction for me is to be able to share what I've seen with other people, to inspire other people, to share the wisdom that I have, and help increase their understanding of our ecosystem and our fragile planet."

Unhappiness with what you're doing for any length of time will affect your overall happiness significantly. It is essential to find a job that not only gives you pleasure but also long-term happiness if you want to live a fulfilled life.

For Schoscho Rufener, "Happiness is more the path; it's an everyday dance between all the contrasts in life: good, bad, feeling well, feeling irritated, and step by step getting on a new level of emotional mastery. If someone has depression and you tell them you must be happier, that will never work." He fully believes you must always experience life at your own pace with new environments, ideas, or models. "It's in the step-by-step approach that people can find a way of magical self-confidence; it's much more than self-calm, it's self-love, it's accepting themselves, getting out of their own way, and leaving aside their burdens. And why not, experience happiness."

Schoscho Rufener shared that at this time in his life, he tries to live every moment in a way that he is nourished and fulfilled on the entire spectrum, from the intellectual to the soul part, feeling at ease, feeling challenged, feeling protected, and nourishing others at the same time. "Because it's our responsibility to be a much more flourishing adult, to enjoy all the complexities of life, in ourselves and our character. I think that's a privilege and a gift, and the further you go on this journey, there is a good chance that you will inspire, motivate, or trigger other people?"

Happiness is a continuous cycle. If you stay in a positive mindset more often, you can enjoy more of the moments you have, whether that's at work, when you talk to people, or when you surround yourself with the right projects and partners. Begin living in the present and not compromising when it comes to your work and the people you stay connected with. Actively seek out the best experiences to enrich your life. All these strategies will help you generate even more happiness.

"Happiness is not something ready-made. It comes from your own actions."

— Dalai Lama

LET'S REVIEW

This chapter is the culmination of everything you've learned in this book: integrating your physical, mental, and spiritual selves in such a way that you begin to live a life of happiness. Remember that this happiness is not the fleeing burst of joy in obtaining possessions, savouring a great meal, or having fun at a party. Instead, we are talking about a lasting feeling of happiness that allows you to live with quiet confidence in yourself and others, optimistic and excited about the future - while remaining grounded in the present. When you embark on this type of journey toward happiness, you will encounter a brighter, more exciting and rewarding world, from relationships to your business. And isn't that what we all crave: a purpose-driven life of no regrets, fulfilling work and relationships, and connection with something greater than ourselves? This is what we believe, and if you got this far with us, we know you believe this, too.

WHAT'S NEXT

We now ask YOU that question. What's next for you? What will you take from this book and apply to your life? What pieces of your life have fallen into place as you reflected and acted on your realisations after reading each chapter? The next page of your "life" book is blank; we hope that you fill those pages with peace, love, success, prosperity, connection . . . and happiness.

Imagine life as a grand orchestra, where each area - your body, your mind, your soul, and all your emotions; your relationships; your career; your personal growth; your impact in the world - is an instrument contributing to the symphony of existence. In this analogy, happiness becomes the melody, the harmonious blend of all these elements playing in sync. Just as a skilled conductor balances the various sections to create a beautiful composition, so must we orchestrate our lives, nurturing each aspect to create a harmonious whole. When every area resonates in harmony, happiness emerges as the sublime music that infuses our daily lives with joy and fulfilment.

Our Deepest Gratitude to Our Contributors

To the successful entrepreneurs whose invaluable wisdom and rich experiences have contributed to the essence of this book, we extend our deepest appreciation. Your unwavering support and inspiring insights have illuminated every chapter of this book. Each conversation, shared experience, and lesson learned together has enriched not only the words within these pages but also our lives.

Thank you for sharing your hearts, minds, and spirits with us as we embarked on this adventure together!

Our wholehearted gratitude to Georg Graf von Walderdorff and Walid Abboud, for their generous support for EnOne, the venture that fuelled this book. We are immensely grateful for your trust, belief, and financial investment.

Thank you for being the incredible individuals who have made this journey possible!

To our talented team of creative minds: our art director Zeynep Burcu Tokatli, our graphic designers Philip Behrends, and Florin Darie, and our editing team led by Howard VanEs - we give our heartfelt gratitude. The artistry and dedication you've poured into your roles have transformed our vision into reality and elevated this project.

Thank you for sharing your expertise, vision, and boundless creativity with us!

Contributing Entrepreneurs

ALINA
LAZARESCU-ABBOUD

Alina Lazarescu-Abboud is a leading Wealth Integration Expert known for her effective methods in assisting Ultra-High-Net-Worth (UHNW) families to successfully adapt to their wealth.

At the heart of her work is metta-morphosys - a proprietary innovative system she designed to aid UHNW individuals and their families in overcoming the psychological, emotional, relational, and economical challenges associated with wealth. Through her method, clients work quickly through complex emotions, break free from unhelpful patterns, and develop a more empowered and grounded perspective in handling their affluence. Additionally, she collaborates with MIT to support upgrading the family wealth operating system, defining purpose, and creating alignment.

Alina's academic background is diverse and comprehensive, encompassing economics, a deep interest in psychology, and expertise in accelerated learning. She is licensed in neuro-experiential therapeutic techniques, mindfulness, and personal and systemic coaching, and possesses a unique edge derived from her personal experience within a UHNW family. This firsthand insight enables her to offer profoundly perceptive and empathetic guidance.

Based in London, Alina works with a global clientele, including celebrities and families from the UK, USA, UAE, and Switzerland. She also shares her expert insights as a contributing writer for prestigious publications such as *Forbes*, *Entrepreneur*, etc.

www.wealthable.info

WALID
ABBOUD

After graduating from ESSEC Business School in 1993, Walid Abboud chose the entrepreneurial path, driving on his own from Lebanon to Romania to explore opportunities in the new emerging economies. He co-founded with three friends what would become the A&D Pharma Group. This venture grew to be the premier pharmaceutical wholesaler, a chain of 530 pharmacies, and a specialist in sales and marketing across five Eastern European countries. A&D Pharma made its mark by listing on the London Stock Exchange in 2006 and executed a strategic exit in 2018 when it reached the one billion turnover.

Parallel to A&D Pharma, Walid launched and exited six companies. He continues to be actively engaged in the Cambridge School of Bucharest, the largest British school in Romania, and Inframappa USA, a pioneering map-based infrastructure management firm. His entrepreneurial ventures also include Babysentry, the market leader ERP for fertility clinics, Simplu Credit in the microcredit sector, and two food supplement businesses in Romania and Spain. 3 start-ups are on the way.

At 54, Walid is a happy husband, with three young children, embracing life with an insatiable curiosity. His passions include music, modern spirituality, and enjoying nature and friendships.

LILA BEHR

Lila, born in Costa Rica and raised across Costa Rica, Germany, and Switzerland, epitomizes the essence of social entrepreneurship, focusing on innovation and systemic change. Her multicultural upbringing fueled her passion for sustainable development and a regenerative economy.

Currently, Lila is developing a unique digital detox retreat center, integrating holistic nutrition and Ayurveda, tailored for CEOs, families, and family offices. This endeavor aligns with her commitment to leading a purpose-first economy.

Her professional roles are diverse and impactful. At Leaders on Purpose, she works as a strategic partnerships and ecosystem associate, guiding multinational corporations towards purpose-centered business practices. Additionally, she serves as community manager for the UNITED PLANET Game, a global platform for visionary leaders and systemic thinkers.

As a passionate social entrepreneur, Lila founded Gaia Protection in Germany and co-founded Gaia Gives, an innovative online fundraising platform designed to enhance the capabilities of social enterprises. She also hosts the Gaia Solutions Podcast, where she highlights significant environmental and social campaigns.

Lila's academic research focuses on the protection of indigenous peoples, people-centered technology, and nature-based solutions. Her work and advocacy extend to philanthropy, women's rights, Agenda 2030, and impact investing, all underlined by her dedication to a purpose-first approach in life and business.

CONSTANTIN BISANZ

Constantin Bisanz is a serial entrepreneur and investor who is currently on a mission to promote spirituality, consciousness, personal transformation, ancient wisdom, and nature conservation. Together with his wife, Evi, they have initiated the Colibri Spirit Festival and Center for Transformation on Corfu Island in Greece.

As a serial entrepreneur and active investor, Constantin has a track record of successfully founding and investing in leading challenger brands in Europe, US, Latin America and Asia. Constantin has been named "Entrepreneur Of The Year" by Harvard Business School and was also named "Exit Champion" for closing Germany's largest Internet exit transaction.

www. colibrispiritfestival.com

ANDREAS E. BRAUCHLIN

Dr. Andreas E. Brauchlin, MD and MSc in economics is a Swiss board-certified specialist in Cardiology, Internal Medicine and Sports Medicine. He is the founder of Swiss Medical Center (SMC), globally renowned as one of the best medical clinics in Switzerland, offering highly individualized services tailored to ensure your personal health not only today but also for the future. As SMC's Medical Director, he is responsible for integrating the most innovative medical technology into the center and expanding its network of global partnerships.

www.swissmedicalcenter.com

HENRY COOKSON

An explorer, conservationist and the Founder of Cookson Adventures, Henry left his career at Goldman Sachs to guide horseback safaris in Kenya, before turning to polar exploration in 2005, and winning the Polar Challenge race to the Magnetic North Pole. Since then, he's set a world record as part of the very first team to reach the South Pole of Inaccessibility without mechanical means and gone on to guide the Walking With The Wounded charity expedition to the North Pole with HRH Prince Harry.

It's these expeditions that served as inspiration in founding Cookson Adventures, bringing the same standards of ground-breaking excellence to the world of private travel. That's whether working with remote tribes in Africa or organising Alaska's most complex charter operations.

Whether it's an epic family adventure or a solo expedition to a remote African tribe or simply some fun in the Scottish Highlands, once Henry knows where your interests lie, he will handcraft the perfect adventure for you. Henry is consistently sought to speak with authority on the cutting edge of global travel and expeditions. Through his work, several million in donations has been raised for charitable causes.

REGULA CURTI

MIA FORBES PIRIE

Musician, Entrepreneur and Philanthropist

Her passion is to create spaces for people to enable consciousness and inner development. She has studied Music and Expressive Arts Therapy (MA) and is trained as a kundalini yoga instructor.

In 2000 on the Lake of Zurich, Regula founded SEESCHAU House of Sacred Arts. Visitors resonate with the clarity and tranquility of the architecture. In the past years many people were invited to experience creative impulses and healing. Moving works of art were created: songs and music compositions, paintings and books, visions of new businesses and products, new life designs and transformations.

In 2007 she and her husband created the non-profit Swiss Beyond Foundation and the project BEYOND MUSIC, a digital platform for musicians of all cultures and genres. More than 50 musical compositions made their way around the world into the hearts of millions of people. Beyond Music unites singers and musicians from different cultures and religions for mutual understanding, love and respect.

In an exciting partnership with other entrepreneurs and Sir Norman Foster, Regula Curti is helping to realize the vision of a co-working hub, a space for time and transformation, in the beautiful valley of the Engadin/Switzerland.

www.innhub.ch
www.beyondmusic.org
www.beyond-foundation.org
www.seeschau.ch

Mia is an award-winning mediator and coach to visionary leaders, teams, and families. Unafraid to broach the issues that many shy away from, she helps people to have transformative conversations and experiences. Since leaving her career as a City of London solicitor in 2007 Mia has worked on a wide range of topics such as business, sustainability, race, gay marriage, and the refugee crisis with clients ranging from the G7 countries and the Government of Mongolia to the Church of England.

Mia's integrative approach, using a variety of techniques, is grounded in her daily meditation practice and annual silent retreats. Her coaching training spans Health, Advanced Narrative and Neuroleadership Coaching. She has also completed all levels of Internal Family Systems Therapy training and trained in couples therapy. Mia teaches facilitation to various clients and institutions and also leads retreats. She is currently working with University College London to help students and the public learn How to Disagree Well and is writing a book on the same topic. Clients at Microsoft have referred to her as "the Einstein of EQ."

www.miaforbespirie.com
www.larespartners.com

GEORG
GRAF VON WALDERDORFF

I had a broad education in various international schools, where I got to know many young people. I was not a good student, but even then I learnt to work creatively.

My business studies were rewarded not only with a good student life but also with a good diploma.

I owe my first encounter with spirituality to my friend and meditation teacher Ralf Wilms, who taught me that there are things between heaven and earth that you can experience but not explain.

My life as an international entrepreneur and working with young start-ups as a start-up angel showed me that flexibility of mind and the will to believe in my goals every day allows me to move mountains and makes me successful.

What all successful people have in common is the ability to keep the gap between decision and execution extremely narrow.

KATJA
BELLINGHAUSEN HENGL

Katja began her career in the 1980s as a classical theater actress in Germany, eventually achieving success in award-winning television shows and movies. She co-founded the 1492 Group in the 1990s and shared her art at the University of Witten/Herdecke in a coaching format she branded "Shakespearience."

This program helps leaders deeply understand who they are, enabling them to outperform in their business roles within their organizations. As a certified teacher of the prestigious Search Inside Yourself Leadership Program, which originated at Google and is based on neuroscience, she conducts international leadership development focusing on enhancing leaders' strategy execution skills.

A significant shift in Katja's work with leaders is helping them realize that the world they experience is invented, not discovered. Katja is also a co-founder of the New School of Business, where business and political leaders are invited to free themselves from their limiting beliefs, learning how to lead their minds first before leading others.

The 21st-century leadership paradigm that Katja and her husband Michael have developed has the potential to shape the world, leading into an era of meta-humanity. In this era, we collectively understand that we transition from scarcity to abundance with self-responsibility as the next-level currency for freedom.

MICHAEL HENGL

Michael became an entrepreneur at nineteen, managing the family business after his career as an Austrian ski racer. His studies include Gestalt Psychology, Integral Philosophy, and Macroeconomics. In 1994, Michael co-founded the 1492 Group and its unique collective intelligence research labs. He lectured on social learning at the University of Witten/Herdecke.

After three decades and over 2000 projects helping companies around the world in 150 countries from USA to China and from Mexico to India, and their leaders to become collectively intelligent, the significant effects on their viability were recognized as a best practice in *Harvard Business Manager*.

The quantum leadership paradigm upon which he has built his work posits that consciousness is not the product of matter, but its cause. Michael experienced that profound spiritual awakening as a teenager himself after a car accident, which literally blew his mind, helping him awaken to reality without filters.

Michael is a scientific author, a blogger for *Harvard Business Review*, a keynote speaker, an investor, and the co-founder and CEO of 1492 Webrain, an AI software facility that transforms from ego to ecosystem for enriching the world.

THOMAS HESSLER

Thomas Hessler is a tech-savvy entrepreneur, investor, and speaker with a passion for emerging technologies and decentralization. He co-founded Zanox, a global leader in performance-based online marketing, and now focuses on empowering young entrepreneurs through mentorship and early-stage investments. A TEDx speaker and a champion of user experience, he is also deeply interested in biohacking, longevity, and the vegan lifestyle.

Thomas is an early adopter of paradigm shifts and innovations, embracing curiosity and creativity in his pursuit of a decentralized world. He believes that the intersection of web3, blockchain, crypto, NFTs, and biohacking will revolutionize the human experience. With his partner, he works on projects that contribute to a better, more sustainable future. Follow him on X.com at @thomashessler

JESSICA HUIE

Jessica Huie MBE is author of *PURPOSE* published by Hay House and founder of Publicity with Purpose. Jessica enjoyed an accomplished career as a publicist and has worked with some of the world's best known stars, entrepreneurs, and personalities.

In 2006 Jessica launched Color Blind Cards, a multi-award winning multicultural greeting card company which drove an early conversation around the importance of ethnic representation in retail and became the first independent brand to secure a high-street presence for black cards.

Labelled one of Britain's Most Inspiring Entrepreneurs by the *Evening Standard*, in 2014 Jessica was honoured with an MBE for entrepreneurship and her contribution to diversity.

https://www.jessicahuie.com
https://www.linkedin.com/in/jessicahuie/

MIKHAIL KOKORICH

Mikhail Kokorich is a European Entrepreneur and Physicist known for his achievements in aeronautical and space-related technologies. Raised in Siberia, Mr. Kokorich continued his education at the Specialized Educational Scientific Center and the NSU Department of Physics. He continued his studies by completing the Stanford Executive Program. He also earned an M.B.A. from the Moscow School of Management. Mr. Kokorik began his journey as an entrepreneur 1997 by founding his first company, Dauria, which provided services to the mining and construction industry. He then moved into space technology, founding companies such as Dauria Aerospace, Astro Digital, Momentus Space, and Destinus. Most notably, Kokorich rose to prominence as the C.E.O. and founder of Momentus, a space transportation company that achieved significant success, including the 2019 NASA iTech Prize and raising $247 million in an I.P.O. In 2021, he will mark another milestone in his pioneering career by founding Destinus, a Swiss company focused on developing hydrogen-powered hypersonic aviation.

DANIEL KRAUSS

As co-founder and chief information officer at Flix, Daniel Krauss manages the company's technology and HR.

Together with his co-founders, he developed Flix as an international transport provider. Krauss is also an investor and member of advisory boards such as uvex. He is convinced that education, entrepreneurship, and innovation can substantially advance humanity. He is a lecturer at FriedrichAlexander University in Erlangen-Nürnberg and a founding partner of the FightBack initiative, which promotes change towards a more sustainable society. He is also an active shareholder in Germany's largest NGO for entrepreneurial education, STARTUP TEENS.

www.flix.com

LAWRENCE LEUSCHNER

Lawrence Leuschner is a German entrepreneur, environmentalist, and philanthropist who builds companies that prioritize sustainability. He is currently the CEO and co-Founder of Europe's largest micromobility provider, TIER Mobility SE. From 2004 to 2017, Leuschner was the CEO of ReBuy GmbH (formerly, Trade-a-game GmbH), an online marketplace for re-purposing used electronics. In 2020, he founded Blue Impact Ventures, a venture capital fund that invests in emerging impact businesses that focus on climate change, public health, democracy-building, nutrition, and sustainable transport. In 2020, Leuschner signed the Founders Pledge, committing 100% of his shares in TIER Mobility to fund climate solutions through Blue Impact Ventures.

SCHOSCHO RUFFENER

Born 1964, he studied economics at St. Gallen University and scenography at the Saint Martins School of Arts, London.

Being the born entrepreneur and a devoted observer of trends in society and economics, he soon started building various ventures mainly in entertainment, events, and lifestyle. A dominant role in his work became Rufener Events, the event agency he founded in 1999 and later sold to MCH group in 2009. Rufener Events is a leading event organizing agency throughout the world with offices in several countries.

Schoscho has worked in more than 70 countries all over the world. His portfolio of equity holdings includes top bars and restaurants in the area of Zurich, as well as successful entertainment formats and high profile communication agencies. He also engaged as a board member of WORLD.MINDS. In 2000, he founded Mountain Wisdom. Mountain Wisdom is a 'by invitation only' community of CEOs, Entrepreneurs and top Executives who meet on a regular basis to share questions, experiences, and answers on career and life.

DAVID WETTON

David helps leaders reach the fulfilment and success they aspire to, through understanding and embodying conscious leadership. He empowers leaders to strike their perfect balance between their inner spiritual expression and outer business ambition.

The leadership teams he works with, report an increase in trust and collaboration; a growth in collective emotional intelligence and a commitment to taking a stand for social impact, alongside delivering excellent financial results.

David holds an MBA from Warwick Business School and qualified as a Chartered Accountant with EY. He is also an ordained UK interfaith minister and spiritual counsellor; which means that he's committed to holding a safe, heartfelt compassionate space for all those he works with.

www.linkedin.com/in/dwetton/

Illustration Credits

Illustrations have been created using
MidJourney and DALL-E 2 by the talented:

Zeynep Burcu Tokatli Page: 8, 14-15, 24, 34-35, 37, 46-47, 54-55, 56, 120-121,
44, 162, 170, 178, 222-223, 244-245, 250.

Philip Behrends Page: 27, 31, 32, 38, 42, 45, 48, 50, 59, 60, 64, 66, 73, 74,
76-77, 78, 83, 85, 86, 88, 93, 94, 100-101, 104, 106,
107, 108, 111, 116, 117, 118, 122, 125, 126, 130, 132,
134, 137, 138, 140, 142, 143, 148, 152, 155, 159,
160, 166-167, 174, 176, 181, 184, 189, 190, 194,
96-197, 200, 203, 204, 207, 210, 214, 217, 219, 224,
228, 231, 233, 235, 236, 239, 241, 246, 249, 252,
255, 257, 260, 263, 266-267.

Photos Page: 28 – A billboard on Times Square announces the merger
between Barça Media and Mountain & Co. I Acquisition Corp.
80 – Conny Boersch with Guido Westerwelle
99 – Conny Boersch on the stage at Unternehmertag in 2022
146 – Conny Boersch
172 – Unicorn Summit at Unternehmertag in 2021
226 – Conny Boersch with his father, Manfred Boersch
262 – Conny Boersch with Gaur Gopal Das at Unternehmertag in 2018